THANKS*GIVING

STEWARDSHIP SERMONS OUT OF THE ETHNIC MINORITY EXPERIENCE

Edited by
J. LaVon Kincaid, Sr.

Sixteen pastors—Asian, Black, Hispanic, and Native American—preach on stewardship themes out of their various Christian traditions.

DISCIPLESHIP RESOURCES　　　　　　　　**NASHVILLE**

Unless otherwise indicated, all scriptural quotations are taken from the Revised Standard Version of the Holy Bible.

ISBN: 0-88177-007-8

Library of Congress Catalog Card Number: 83-73266

THANKS*GIVING: STEWARDSHIP SERMONS OUT OF THE ETHNIC MINORITY EXPERIENCE. Copyright © 1984 by Discipleship Resources. All rights reserved. Printed in the United States of America. No part of this book may be reproduced in any manner whatsoever without written permission except in the case of brief quotations embodied in critical articles or reviews. For information address Discipleship Resources, P. O. Box 840, Nashville, TN 37202.

This book is dedicated to my family—

Bobi, LaMar, J. LaVon, Jr., and
mother, Louise

CONTENTS

Foreword—*Bishop Melvin G. Talbert* vi
Preface—*Thomas C. Rieke* viii
Introduction—*J. LaVon Kincaid, Sr.* x

STEWARDSHIP IS ENTRUSTING OUR LIVES TO GOD
The Battle for High Ground—*Leonard L. Haynes, Jr.* 1
The Bamboo Tree—*Jung Young Lee* 7
Our Sufficiency Is of God—*Everett S. Reynolds, Sr.* 12
God's Sovereignty—*Víctor Bonilla* 16

STEWARDSHIP IS CARING FOR OTHER PERSONS
A Stewardship of Service—*Richard Matsushita* 21
Stewardship: A Call to Liberation—*Russell F. McReynolds* 24
Gather up the Fragments—*John Joong Tai Kim* 29
Weep No More, My Lady—*Jun Ehara* 35

STEWARDSHIP IS USING OUR GIFTS FAITHFULLY
The Stewardship of Life's Leftovers—*Zan W. Holmes, Jr.* 40
Such as I Have—*Mary Lou Santillán Baert* 45
Blessings That Come through Shortages—*Edward E. Bufford* 49
What to Do (and Not Do) When in Financial Trouble—
  Roberto Escamilla 53

STEWARDSHIP IS GIVING AS WE HAVE RECEIVED
Costly Giving—*Joseph B. Bethea* 58
The Stewardship of Money—*David Adair* 62
Giving as Sacrificial Sharing—*Norval I. Brown* 66
Is God in Your Budget?—*J. LaVon Kincaid, Sr.* 70

Foreword

Bishop Melvin G. Talbert

After many years of talking about the idea and hoping something could be done, we finally have a collection of sermons in which is expressed our commitment to Christian stewardship from the perspective of ethnic minorities. Because of their racial and cultural uniqueness, the approach of ethnic minorities to stewardship differs from that of the ethnic majority.

Certainly this volume should become a major and valuable addition to the many stewardship resources available currently. It should serve to enlighten our vision and to broaden our understanding of this most essential subject. Most important, it should affirm the fact that ethnic minorities have a significant contribution to make in stewardship—an essential aspect of our life and mission.

Several years ago, a professional staff person of a general agency of a church said to me, "Ethnic minorities do not know how to do stewardship." Such a statement was shortsighted and incorrect, to say the least. A serious reading of the sermons within this volume will quickly dispel that type of thinking. Stewardship has to do with more than raising money. Stewardship encompasses all that we do in making proper use of the material and human resources placed in our care.

It is true, however, that an important aspect of stewardship is raising money in our churches. Here the situation with many ethnic minority persons is different. Most ethnic minorities live on marginal incomes. Survival is a constant challenge. Therefore, to assume that the only way to raise money is to conduct a pledge campaign and build the budget accordingly is unrealistic. In most instances ethnic minority congregations project "faith budgets" and imaginative ways to augment pledges through funding programs and events. I hope we have arrived at a time when such approaches to stewardship are recognized as authentic means of reaching out in service to God and to humanity. If this is the case, then this volume may serve as a celebration of that achievement.

It is my hope that clergy and laity of all racial and cultural backgrounds, Anglo and non-Anglo, will read this volume. I believe all will find these sermons on stewardship enlightening, challenging, and inspiring.

A word of commendation is due the Reverend J. LaVon Kincaid, Sr., a staff member of the Section on Stewardship, Board of Discipleship, The United Methodist Church, for his persistence and resourcefulness in seeing this project through to completion.

Melvin G. Talbert, Bishop
The United Methodist Church
The Seattle Area
Seattle, Washington

Preface

Thomas C. Rieke

There are still people who will affirm with the ancient writer, "There is nothing new under the sun." You may be one of those persons. But please don't look for me in that group. I am simply not a believer!

I might have been of that persuasion at one time. But if I had been, it was before The United Methodist Church adopted as its missional priority for 1980-84, Developing and Strengthening the Ethnic Minority Local Church. As I thought about that action, it dawned on me that the discipline of Christian stewardship was likely to be the bridge over which significant crossings might occur between churches of differing ethnic backgrounds. So the idea was put to the test.

To facilitate the process, staff members of the Section on Stewardship, Board of Discipleship, sat down on separate occasions with representatives of each of the four major ethnic groupings of The United Methodist Church—Asian, Black, Hispanic, and Native American. The aim was to listen as persons spoke about their perceptions of stewardship. I, for one, was persuaded that something new was happening—for me and likely for others.

The gospel came alive again. This time it was in the eyes and hearts and experiences of persons of other races. They told an old story in ways that were fresh and new and exciting. They used new words and touching experiences and relevant history to make the gospel live again.

The occasion revealed several new insights in stewardship. For instance, we learned that our Hispanic friends viewed *giving* as a responsible way of life. Black Christians marched around the subject like Joshua at Jericho and brought down the barriers, opening the subject to fresh inspection. Blacks see stewardship as *grateful response* to God's will. Native Americans see stewardship as *wholeness* in life. They look at contemporary patterns of living through eyes that view Creation as divine and see the lack of Christian stewardship in those patterns. Asian Americans with lighthearted seriousness view stewardship as *caring* for all of the gifts of life.

Nothing new? Don't you believe it for a minute longer. Read on and find the story of stewardship as seen through the varied experiences of preachers who speak in the chapters of this book. Yours too will be the joy of seeing something fresh and new in a rich and familiar story.

J. LaVon Kincaid, Sr., is a student of stewardship in the context of the Christian faith. He has experienced it for himself, knows whereof he speaks, and is open to fresh insights and truth. He is a member of the staff of The United Methodist Church's Section on Stewardship and a valued colleague. He has been eyes and ears of ethnicity for those of us who work with him. He is patient and growing and caring in all of his relationships. It was his vision that perceived this book and his persistence that brought it into being. Those of us who labor with him salute him.

Books of sermons come and go. Perhaps that fate will befall this volume some day. But if it does, it will not happen until that day when the world will have seen the fulfillment of the New Testament perspective: "Because your connection with Christ makes you one with each other, in your society there can be no Jew or Greek, no slave or free man, no male or female" (Gal. 3:28, Barclay).

When that day arrives, sermons will become moot. Until then, read on to your profit and your salvation!

Thomas C. Rieke
General Board of Discipleship
Nashville, Tennessee

INTRODUCTION

J. LaVon Kincaid, Sr.

It is with humility and honor that we share this book of stewardship sermons in the ethnic minority tradition. By "ethnic minority" we mean Asian and Pacific Islanders, Blacks, Hispanics, and Native Americans. Although there are other minority groups within the church, we shall confine our treatment to only these mentioned here.

Preaching is central to the Christian faith and tradition. This is especially true within the ethnic minority church. Moreover, because minority persons are more oral than literary, preaching becomes one of the primary vehicles by which the faith, tradition, and theology are communicated and passed on to future generations. Preaching takes on a positive and dominant role in the overall religious experience of the ethnic minority local church. Stewardship is among the main subjects preached in the minority church tradition. Others include evangelism, salvation, the love of God, and liberation, to mention only a few.

The common thread which binds most minorities together is that of "oppression." For the most part, ethnic minorities are the "rejected, powerless, outcast, and oppressed" people of our society and the world. Oppression is the one experience that constitutes a most dynamic and unique reality of minority life. This unique fact, combined with others, points to the need for the development of a "theology of hope and liberation" by the church. Preaching stewardship is one of the ways in which the theology of hope and liberation is communicated.

In this book, you will discover several expressions of minority stewardship and theology that are unique. The minority life experience in North America is mainly a struggle for survival. Survival is the dominant theme of life for the average minority person. How survival takes place within the context of the Christian faith is important to the stewardship of life for the believer.

In his book, *God's Trombones*, James Weldon Johnson says, "Preaching is synonymous with hearing a word straight from heaven." That word is a word of hope and life in a land where survival is so important and death is always a reality. To hear the preached word, the "good news," is the main purpose of the congregation in coming together from week to week, month to month. Second only to preaching is the strong bond of fellowship, portrayed through singing, praying, confession, witness, and other acts of corporate worship and celebration.

Preaching stewardship is an accepted practice within most minority churches. Preachers take very seriously the opportunity to preach sermons on stewardship. The stewardship of the preacher's ministry compels him or her to preach on the subject of stewardship and all of its aspects. Particularly is this true as it relates to preaching on subjects such as time and abilities, love, financial support, Christian service, tithing, and the stewardship of managing well the resources God has entrusted to our care.

To understand and appreciate stewardship and proclamation in the minority context, one needs to experience the richness of a worship service in one of the Black, Hispanic, Asian, or Native American churches. So much can be learned from such an experience. For example, one learns that preaching takes on a variety of exciting and distinct forms in each of the four groups. Additionally, social and economic standing of the people affects how stewardship is preached in each of these churches. For instance, in the middle- to upper-class churches, preachers tend to be rather reserved in preaching stewardship. While in the middle to lower socioeconomic class, one finds stewardship being preached rather freely, and the subject of money embraced more easily.

Most preachers take seriously the words of Paul the apostle as recorded in 1 Corinthians 9:16, "Woe to me if I do not preach the gospel," and 2 Timothy 4:2, "Preach the word, be urgent in season and out of season." The minority preacher is expected to give clear directions to the congregation as to how to improve their personal and group lifestyle as he or she declares, "Thus says the Lord."

Minority stewardship sermons, for the most part, are biblically based, theologically grounded, and textually sound. They usually take the form of storytelling. The stories generally relate to the culture and life experience of the people. Stories are best remembered by the people, and are, therefore, effective in communication of stewardship ideas and concepts.

Stewardship proclamation is usually dramatic and exciting. The sermon may be met by verbal exclamations by the congregation— "Amen," "Praise the Lord," "Hallelujah!" This is known as "the call and response method" of preaching. While it is not true of all minority churches, it is rather widespread throughout North America. However, the higher the socioeconomic level of the congregation, the less emotional is its worship.

The congregation expects the preacher to capture the ear and imagination of the worshipers, to inspire and encourage them to sound stewardship practices. Sermons that "lift up bowed-down heads" are the best loved and the most effective. The purpose of preaching stewardship is, after all, to inspire and motivate members to proper actions in their personal stewardship. Texts are generally on stewardship themes and may be taken from a wide range of material from Genesis (the Creation story), to Revelation (the Last Judgment and the New Creation). Whether it be on money, time usage, talents, or other pertinent aspects of stewardship, the preacher is quite bold and straightforward in breaking the spiritual bread.

Many sermons center around God's gracious acts of love, mercy, and blessings. The steward is encouraged to respond to God's goodness through acts of thanks-giving, which is good stewardship on the part of the Christian disciple.

Another important aspect of preaching stewardship is in the way in which minority pastors give personal leadership in both the church and community. Effectively "pastoring the flock" is stewardship in action. Many pastors are effective as leaders because of their own personal and family stewardship practices. Generally pastors set the tone and level of stewardship within the congregation. The pastor is the key steward. The people generally follow where led.

What we shall see in the sermons that follow are examples of special features and characteristics of minority church stewardship in sermonizing forms. As you read these sermons, there are several important things to look for: (a) how the sermon is begun, generally in storytelling form, (b) how the central theme of the sermon is presented, (c) how the text is followed, (d) the challenge to commitment, and (e) creativity by pastors regarding the text and subject.

It is our sincere hope that this work will be helpful and informative to all who read and reflect upon these pages. It is further hoped that this work will in some small way meet a need within the church at large, and that this work is spiritually uplifting and inspiring to you. May the gift of the Holy Spirit be your guide.

Special thanks and sincere appreciation are lovingly expressed to all who helped to make the dream of this publication a reality. Many long and dedicated hours have gone into bringing our hopes, dreams, and goals to their fruition. Thanks be to God!

I wish to express special thanks and appreciation to my loving wife, Bobi, for her encouragement and affirmation in supporting me to the project's end, and for her warmth, understanding, and input throughout the project. Also, to our two sons, Lamar and LaVon, Jr., special thanks for their support and love.

Many thanks to my colleagues in the Section on Stewardship staff, Thomas C. Rieke, Albert Hooke, and William Miller, for their extra efforts and labor of love assisting in the editing of each sermon.

Thanks to all who took time to write and submit sermons for this publication. Indeed, all of these men and women are God's choice stewards. Thanks to our faithful and efficient secretaries, Mary Boyd and Wanda Louise Bumpus, for their expert typing and personal input, and for going beyond the call of duty in the typing and advising of each sermon.

I wish to thank the following persons who served as consultants, along with many others who are too many to acknowledge here. May God bless each of you.

Dr. John Corry
Reverend Sang E. Chun
Dr. Richard Eslinger
Dr. Roberto Escamilla
Dr. Hoyt Hickman
Reverend Leo H. Hsu
Dr. Major J. Jones
Reverend Mamie Ko
Reverend David Long, Jr.

Dr. Hugo López
Dr. Russell McReynolds
Dr. Marcus Matthews
Dr. James C. Peters
Ms. Teresa Santillán
Bishop Melvin G. Talbert
Reverend Theo Triplett
Ms. Becky Thompson
Ms. Dorothy Turner-Lacy

Shalom,
J. LaVon Kincaid, Sr.
Director of Stewardship
Board of Discipleship
Nashville, Tennessee

THE BATTLE FOR HIGH GROUND

Leonard L. Haynes, Jr.
Baton Rouge, Louisiana

Text: To Thee, O Lord, I lift up my soul (Psalm 25:1).

Biographical Sketch

Leonard L. Haynes, Jr., a Black United Methodist minister, was born in Austin, Texas. He was educated at Huston-Tillotson College, where he received the B.A. degree. He received the Master of Divinity from Gammon Theological Seminary of Atlanta, Ga., and the Doctor of Sacred Theology from Boston University.

Presently he is pastor of Wesley United Methodist Church in Baton Rouge, Louisiana where he has served for over twenty years. Dr. Haynes is also professor of philosophy at Southern University. Listed among the Ten Outstanding Men in Baton Rouge, in Who's Who in America, he is the author of several publications and articles.

Dr. Haynes is a distinguished former President of Morristown College, Morristown, Tennessee. He has traveled widely over two-thirds of the world and is well known for his outstanding preaching.

Dr. Haynes and his wife live in Baton Rouge, Louisiana.

There are few of us who have not had the desire for high ground. Such desires of the human spirit are nurtured in the warp and woof of life's situations, circumstances, and experiences. Desires of the spirit are and can be tremendous assets if disciplined and nurtured. But if left alone and unbridled, they can become sources of tumultuous and devastating hardships. Desires, however, are normal and when elevated by the stewardship of service, time, talent, and giving, they become sources which aid in the battle for life's high ground. Higher ground represents the best possible state a Christian can reach while here on earth.

One of the great hymns in the *Songs of Zion* hymnbook is the beloved hymn of the Black Christian experience, "Lord Plant My Feet on Higher Ground." This great hymn expresses the desire and attitude of many stewards and Christian disciples to reach the personal and spiritual goal of "higher ground."

There are several approaches one can take in the pursuit of higher ground. For our purpose here we shall only mention three.

First, Western monasticism has profited by a long tradition of piety and controlled discipline, as a means by which the battle for higher ground can be seized and fulfilled. Christendom with its scripture, tradition, and experience sprang out of the longing of a monastic search, beginning in the Middle East and later Africa, for a corporate reality which in many instances sustained, preserved, and created the best in Christian civilization throughout the known world. A life lived with bridled charity, chastity, and poverty, has seen high moments in the renewal of the human spirit.

Bernard of Clairvaux sings, "Jesus, thou joy of loving hearts, Thou fount of life, Thou light of men! From the best bliss that earth imparts, We turn unfilled to thee again." Saint Francis of Assisi thrills us later with the love of nature, Brother Son, Sister Moon, Mother Earth, coupled with unmatched service and charity to human life.

This mood is expressed also in the tradition, experience, beauty, and splendor of the Black slave in America. The Black slave worshiper has provided a remarkable lineage of subdued and more relaxed affirmation of being in the world as well as American society. The nobility of the human spirit seen in the sorrow song and life of the early Black fathers and mothers, whose love of God and the church led a great preacher, by the name of Howard Thurman, to write the book, *Jesus and the Disinherited*. "You can have all of this world, but give me Jesus," is the battle cry of the Black slave in search of higher ground in a competitive society of unbridled passion. This cry is a source of grace and dignity in the human battle for high ground.

The second attitude frequently expressed by the volcanic eruptions of the sensate culture in which we live is to fling our control of human desires to the wind. This means seeking high ground by doing what one wants to and what one pleases to do, anywhere, any place, any time. This is referred to as "doing one's thing." Is there no wonder that lives reflected around us and displayed by television and radio commercials can leave us with this attitude as the higher value of the human soul?

The Greek philosopher Epictetus said, "Eat, drink, and be merry for tomorrow you may die." The Persian philosopher Omar Khayam said, "O if I but with Thee could conspire to grasp these sorry schemes of things entire, would we not shatter them into bits and hold them nearer to the heart's desires." The wreckage of human history and life in both young and old reveals that undisciplined desires will lead us to moments of grief—and finally to unfulfilled longing in the battle for the ground of the free spirit and the human soul. "Lord, plant my feet on higher ground."

The third approach to seizing the high ground of the human soul is to take one's desires and lay them upon the highest tribunal of the soul, the altar of God. David, "the sweet singer of tunes," leads us in the 25th Psalm to a clearer vision of "the good, the true, the beautiful," when he suggests in the first verse, "To Thee, O Lord, I lift up my soul." Finding self-enrichment, self-fulfillment, by taking one's desires and placing them on the altar of God is the means which led him through "life's changing scenes" to high ground.

The altar of God as found in the church, the place of our father and mother, the shelter of the meek and the lowly, the arbiter of justice between the rich and the poor, the place where the "wicked cease from troubling and the weary can be at rest," our rock in a weary land, our shelter in the time of storm—this altar can be found to be a source of satisfying strength and hope. At the altar of God, one can commit talents and resources and treasures which have been given by God as a trust. On the altar of God, one can place time, one's historicity, and even death with its possibility in order to avoid emptiness and meaninglessness in a ceaseless flux of events. "Take time to be holy," becomes a reverence for human life wherever it can be found.

Stewardship finds meaning at the altar of God. Here is *the high ground,* the end of longings and desires the penitent seeks to find. The altar of God takes the "weary traveler" beyond the life of sensate and sensory culture. The altar voids our attachment to the material affections of the world as a source of joy. One's commitment brings into meaningful control the human heart. The altar lifts up sacrifice as the noble virtue by which the world can become a part of the immediately seen, while giving at the same time the eternal and unseen.

There are some suggestions, yea, admonitions that will need to be fulfilled. One does not just walk into a treasury of fulfilled desires without refining the human spirit with the character of Christlike faith. Let me suggest at least three ways in which the human spirit can express stewardship with a Christlike faith.

Number one, a sense of dedication. What a unique moment when the spirit can be dedicated to a high purpose. What a great resource and inspiration to see the dedication of great Black men and women such as Booker T. Washington, who left Hampton Institute and built Tuskegee Institute in Alabama; a slave by the name of George Washington Carver, who was sold for a mule, but built an institute of noble worth and shared scientific insights that saved the South, also at Tuskegee. Carver's gifts to the world, given without charge and cost, left the scientific world amazed. As he frequently proclaimed, "What I have given to the world, God gave them to me."

What tremendous dedication is seen in the rich moments of selflessness as reflected in the musical art of Roland Hayes, Marion Anderson, Leontyne Price. Or in Bishop Willis J. King in Biblical Study at Gammon Theological Seminary in Atlanta, or Bishop Robert E. Jones, founder and builder of Gulfside Methodist Assembly in Waveland, Mississippi. The stewardship of Mary McCleod Bethune, founder of Bethune-Cookman College in Daytona Beach, Florida, is most outstanding. She gave of her time, talent, and finances in order to reach her goals, the establishment of a college for Black youth, "higher ground." Rev. J. LaVon Kincaid, Sr. in his book, *God's Faithfulness: Stewardship in the Ethnic Minority Local Church*, states, "The task of the Christian steward . . . is to witness through word, deed, gift and service to the work of Christ."

Souls who have climbed to higher ground through dedication are numbered in the millions on the sands of the sea of time. They are there as a witness and challenge to us all. They are not to be forgotten, because their contribution is great. They are our Black forefathers and mothers, from the time of slavery, back to our African genesis, to the very present moment.

We cannot forget the Sunday school teachers, the church school superintendents, the choir directors, the saints who through prayer and close contact with God, through dedicated desires, raise us to the mountaintops of the human spirit. They stretch themselves out and by faith lead us to a higher glory. The Black church has seen these souls whom God loved "keep on toiling"—toiling through the sun, storm, and rain—trying to make a hundred because ninety-nine and one-half would not do!

The creative way in life in which desires can be expressed is through "consecration." Fanny J. Crosby sang, "Consecrate me now to thy service Lord by the power of grace divine, Let my soul look up with a steadfast hope and *my will* be lost in thine." Consecration is greater than dedication. Consecration makes us move closer and closer to the living God and charges us in the brokenness of the world to "get up on our feet" and share the burden of God by bringing human life close to him.

When Richard Allen, of Philadelphia, was dragged from the altar of St. George Methodist Episcopal Church and thrown into the street on his face, he looked back and looked up to God, and said to himself, "I must get up." O friends, isn't this what a consecrated life in our time ultimately does? When in the brokenness of life and in our own fragmented world we look at the battle of life and find ourselves on our faces, with limited resources round about us, we rise with the power of God and say to ourselves, "We must get up." In getting up, Allen led his people in the founding of Mother Bethel African Methodist Episcopal Church, and a new Black Methodist denomination.

Reverend Richard Allen's acts of stewardship have challenged every Black in some way to a higher level of personal stewardship. Blacks have been inspired and motivated to overcome conditions of physical and psychological slavery. They have come to grips with the twentieth century with a consecrated life, saying, " "I must get up." Wasn't this also the experience of a Bedouin people recorded in Israel's history? Time and again, prostrate and on their knees, "Way down yonder by myself, when I couldn't hear nobody pray," there came the inspiration of a consecrated life, through a judge, a seer, a prophet, telling the nation that "they must get up."

Another moment comes so great, "I scarce can take it in," when Jesus Christ, Mary's Baby, Dying Lamb, Rose of Sharon, Bright and Morning Star, was brought to his knees in the brokenness of the Garden of Gethsemane, and cried aloud, "If I lay this body down, I will also take it up." Down the arena of time a continuous call comes from our Lord and Master. Through human, Godlike moments, it fills our souls in churches today to "get up and get on" with the Master's business. That business is our faithful stewardship.

We stand in the need of confession for our lack of consecration: "Not my brother, not my sister, but it's me, O Lord, standing in the need of prayer."

This leads us to our final quest for God's high ground. Dedication and consecration are simply steps by which we can move forward and do God's will.

The great man from Atlanta by the name of Martin Luther King, Jr., gave us in the climax of his life in Memphis a word to challenge when he said, "I've been to the mountaintop; I've seen the Promised Land. I may not get there with you, but one day, my people will be free." Such a vision of God's will is not only the story of Martin Luther King, Jr., but that matchless line of splendor that ends in the greatest moment of the human spirit found also in the Christ that forgives and seeks to save the lost.

The cross is the final triumph over tragedy that leads us to higher ground and brings us to this moment. Those of us who have been forgiven extend ourselves to the world and the events that call us to do God's will.

Several years ago, I was delayed at the gates of Nairobi, Kenya, because I had left my passport in another bag. Making the most of that moment I said to the officer, "I do not have my passport, but I am a brother, may I pass?" He simply said, "Passport, please." I said, "But I know Martin Luther King, Jr." His reply, "Passport, please." Finally, I told him where it was and he assisted me in retrieving the passport for entrance.

How many of us will get to the gates of glory and seek to enter—only to hear the guide say, "Passport, please" Our reply can easily be one of frustration as we flitter with undisciplined desires and frustrations by saying, "My mother and father and sister and brother are great church workers"—but the guide will simply say again, "Passport, please."

Jesus in that marvelous moment in the Book of Matthew gives us a clue to what our stewardship finally means as he calls our attention to the Last Judgment scene: "For I was an hungered, and ye gave me meat: I was thirsty, and ye gave me drink: I was a stranger, and ye took me in: Naked, and ye clothed me: I was sick, and ye visited me: I was in prison, and ye came unto me. . . . And the King shall answer and say unto them, Verily I say unto you, Inasmuch as ye have done it unto one of the least of these my brethren, ye have done it unto me" (KJV).

For this we give thanks, that those whom we have known and loved "longer since and lost awhile" were tested in the fires of life and battled through the spurious and the uncertain desires until they found their sure footing on higher ground. "To Thee, O Lord, I lift up my soul." Through these persons, we join our testing in the fires of life and battle to attain higher ground. Amen.

THE BAMBOO TREE

Jung Young Lee
Grand Forks, North Dakota

Text: Have this mind among yourselves, which is yours in Christ Jesus, who, though he was in the form of God, did not count equality with God a thing to be grasped, but emptied himself, taking the form of a servant, begin born in the likeness of men. And being found in human form he humbled himself and became obedient unto death, even death on a cross (Phil. 2:5-8).

Biographical Sketch

Jung Young Lee is a native of North Korea. He came to America in 1955. Rev. Dr. Lee holds the B.S. in Chemistry from Findlay College in 1957, B.D. from Garrett Theological Seminary in 1961, M.S. in Library Science from Western Reserve University in 1962, and Th.D. from Boston University in 1968.

He is a ministerial member of West Ohio Conference, The United Methodist Church. Dr. Lee is the founder and past president of the Fund for Korean Christian Ministers in Washington, D.C. and the founder and past minister of the Korean Church in Columbus, Ohio.

Dr. Lee has distinguished himself by receiving many honors, including the following: Senior Fulbright-Hays Scholar, teaching at Seoul National University, Ewha Woman's University, Methodist Theological Seminary in Seoul, Otterbein College, San Francisco Theological Seminary, Graduate Theological Union, Iliff School of Theology, and Garrett-Evangelical Theological Seminary. He is the author of a dozen books which include Cosmic Religion (Harper, 1978), Theology of Change (Orbis Books, 1979), and others.

Dr. Lee has published more than forty articles in various journals, such as Journal of Ecumenical Studies, International Review of Mission, Scottish Journal of Theology, and History of Religion.

Presently he is Professor of Religious Studies at the University of North Dakota, minister of the Concrete United Methodist Church, and Coordinator of the Ministerial Task Force for Asian-American Christians in Grand Forks, North Dakota.

Because of my Oriental background I cannot help but be attracted by something peculiarly Oriental in nature. Whenever I see an Oriental picture or Oriental furniture or anything which is Oriental, I have to look at it twice before I pass it by.

Among many trees the bamboo is special to Asians. It is certainly true for me. Whenever I see the bamboo tree, I cannot but admire it. Because I like the bamboo tree, I brought one a few years ago all the way from California to North Dakota. I placed it right next to the door where everyone could easily spot it. My American friends come and often remark that the bamboo gives an Oriental touch to my home. However, they are not especially attracted by it. When my Asian friends come and see the bamboo tree, almost all of them pay extra attention to it with great admiration.

I know that the bamboo means something special to Asians. Why is it? There are many beautiful trees besides the bamboo. Why does the bamboo express the ethos of Asian people? Is it special because it is an evergreen? The pine is also an evergreen tree. Why then is the bamboo different from all other trees? It is special, I think, because *it is hollow*. This emptiness makes the bamboo different from all other trees and gives a special significance to Asians.

I don't know why or how the Oriental people have come to place such value on emptiness. For most Westerners emptiness means very little. But for Asians, emptiness is often more valuable than fullness.

It is said that the Oriental artist usually spends more time and gives more attention to the allocation of empty space than drawing actual paintings. Harmony and tranquility in Oriental arts have a lot to do with the creative use of empty space. We also notice that the basic feature of an Oriental house is emptiness. If you look at the traditional Korean *ondol* room (which is heated from below) or Japanese *tatami* (straw mat) room, you don't see any tables or chairs in it. If the room is not empty, it is useless. Likewise, the value of a bowl or utensil comes from its emptiness. When the bowl is full, it is of no use. Here, emptiness has more value than fullness.

One of the famous temples in Tokyo is the Ryo-an Temple. It is famous because of the empty garden. In the garden you don't see anything but the white sand. Nevertheless, hundreds and hundreds of people visit there every day to see this garden. They stand there to meditate on the empty garden. Emptiness for Asians means more than nothing. It carries a positive value.

We also see the special significance of emptiness in Christianity. According to Paul's Epistle to the Philippians, Christ emptied himself, taking the form of a servant and being born in the likeness of men. This *kenosis* doctrine is one of our finest descriptions of the incarnation of Christ. Christ emptied himself of his glory, the glory of being equal with God. He emptied himself of his power, the almighty power over all things. He emptied himself of his authority to rule the world. By emptying himself of the form of God he was transformed into the form of a servant. This is the true meaning of incarnation. This is the radical transformation of the divine to the human nature. This radical transformation is possible, because Christ emptied himself totally. In other words, God became a man, because he emptied himself of his divine nature.

A master cannot become a servant unless he empties himself of the nature of being a master. This emptying process is essential for a radical transformation. Christ poured out his divine characteristics and was transformed into the lowest category of human existence, that is, the form of servant. To me this is the uniqueness of Christ and the Christian faith. I don't see it in any other religion in the world.

Although the Buddha can be somewhat comparable to Jesus, he has never been considered to be divine. It is true that the Buddha had to renounce all the privileges of being a prince when he became a monk. This is known as the Great Renunciation. However, he didn't take the form of a servant. Rather, he was elevated to the priestly class (or Brahmans) from the ruling class (or Kshatriyas) in Indian society. Christ is unique, because he, by the self-emptying process, transformed himself from the highest of the divine nature to the lowest form of human being. By taking the form of a servant rather than the form of a master, he came to understand the agony of suffering humanity and to empathize with the poor, the oppressed, and the weak. This was then the way of saving the world to himself, and to God.

If you have never been a servant, you may not understand fully what it means to be a servant. I was perhaps fortunate in many ways to have the experience of being both a master and servant. When I was about six years old, our home in Korea was still wealthy enough to have many servants. I had my own servant who was a fifteen-year-old boy. I used to call him *Daeji* or "Pig." Wherever I went, he had to come along. He had to obey me and do whatever I commanded him to do.

I remember very well one day when we went to a mountain not too far away from our home. I saw a beautiful flower on the top of a rugged cliff. I pointed at it and asked my servant to bring it to me. Climbing up the cliff was so dangerous that he almost lost his life. Yet, he had to bring me the flower because he was my servant. On another occasion I fell down on the playground and hurt myself. As a small boy I cried loudly as I was coming into the house. My father was angry at the servant and said, "What were you doing when my son fell down?" He was beaten up by my father, but he could not say a word.

Time passed fast. Soon the Second World War was over and the

Korean War started. In December of 1950 I was among many thousands of war refugees traveling toward the south. I never thought that I would travel all the way to South Korea when I left home. I didn't have any money. I became a penniless refugee in South Korea. I had to beg for food to keep myself alive. I traveled all the way to Milyang city, about seventy miles north of Pusan, and I was taken into a wealthy home where I was hired to be the servant of an old gentleman.

During the three months of my stay with this man I found out what it meant to be a servant. I was the extension of his hands and legs. I had to do exactly and efficiently what my master told me to do. More than that, I had to do what he expected me to do. No matter how much I disagreed with him or how unhappy I was with my work, I could not say a single no to his demands. I was practically his possession. I became his thing, not a person. I didn't have any rights of my own. My entire existence depended on him. If he had wanted to kill me, he certainly could have. I lived under the shadow of fear and uncertainty.

My master demanded of me absolute obedience, obedience even to death. During those days I recalled my servant, "Pig," of my younger days. I came to empathize with those who were oppressed. I learned how inhumane it is to be a servant. Christ became a servant and was obedient even to death, so that all might be liberated from their slavery to sin. To be a servant means to empty oneself of one's right to be a free person. Christ, pouring out his divinity, took up the form of a servant to save the world. This is the essence of the Christian message for us to proclaim.

Being a Christian means to become a servant of God. Therefore, we as Christians must empty ourselves, as Christ did. We need to empty our inside like the bamboo tree. Our mind and heart are full of envy, jealousy, prejudice, arrogance, and self-pride. Unless we empty them from ourselves, we cannot become the instruments of God.

Let me share a story which can help us to understand the importance of emptying our minds. During the Meiji era in Japan (1868-1912), Nan-in was a well known Zen master. One day a university professor visited him to inquire about meditation. As an Oriental custom the master served tea. He poured the cup full, and then kept on pouring. The professor watched the overflowing cup and, greatly disturbed, said, "It is overfull. Stop pouring!" "Like this cup," the master said, "you are full of your thoughts. How can I teach you meditation unless you empty your thought? Empty your cup!" If our minds and hearts are full of past memories, worries, and selfish desires, we cannot receive the Word of God. We cannot receive Christ unless we first empty ourselves. By emptying ourselves we can become the temple of the Holy Spirit.

We remember the Christmas story. There was no room for Jesus in Bethlehem. Every room was crowded, so that Jesus was born in a manger. Like Bethlehem, our hearts and minds are crowded with our own thoughts and desires. We have to make a room for Christ, so that he can be born again and again in us. Certainly, the bamboo is a symbol of Christmas. When we were in California we used the bamboo rather than the pine as our Christmas tree. It was so meaningful to us, because the bamboo tree, being empty inside, represents the incarnation of Christ and the emptiness of our heart and mind, where Christ is born at Christmas.

The bamboo is also known as the symbol of faithfulness, as the faithfulness of a minister to his king. Like other evergreen trees, the bamboo remains faithful and the same even in the cold winter. Moreover, its emptiness is an expression of faith. Like the empty bowl carried by the beggar or a wandering monk, the empty person is totally dependent on the giver. In many Third World countries we see the beggars carrying empty bowls to receive foods. When I was begging for food during the Korean War, I didn't even have an empty bowl to take with me. I had to stretch out my empty hands. I had to wait, wait and wait, until my empty hands were filled up with food.

To be a faithful Christian means to be like the beggar who stretches out his empty hands to God. Our attitude must be always like the empty hand or empty bowl, which God can fill with his love. Our faith is the empty vessel, while God's love is the overflowing content. Our emptying process is the life of faith. Every day we are asked to empty ourselves. Our Christian living is none other than the life of emptying—emptying for God.

As the bamboo tree grows, its inside becomes more hollow. Likewise, our inside has to be emptied more and more as we grow in Christian faith. We have to allow more room for Christ as we mature in Christian life. As the bowl is useful because of its emptiness, we become useful to God when we empty ourselves. Our old selves have to be emptied, so that our new selves may be born with the presence of Christ in us. In this way we are born again and again as we empty ourselves each time. When we completely empty ourselves for Christ, we are united with him. Then, he is in us and we in him. And we can say with Paul, "It is no longer I who live, but Christ who lives in me" (Gal. 2:20).

Amen and praise be unto God.

OUR SUFFICIENCY IS OF GOD

Everett S. Reynolds, Sr.
Kansas City, Missouri

Text: Not that we are sufficient of ourselves to think anything as of ourselves, but our sufficiency is of God (2 Cor. 3:5).

Biographical Sketch

Everett S. Reynolds was born in a Methodist parsonage in St. Louis, Missouri. He grew up and attended several schools in Missouri, and graduated from Omaha Technical High School.

He holds the B.S. degree from Philander College, Little Rock, Arkansas; the Bachelor of Divinity from Eden Theological Seminary, Webster Grove, Missouri; and the Doctor of Theology from the Faith Evangelistic Seminar of Morgantown, Kentucky. Dr. Reynolds has done additional study at the University of Nebraska in Educational Psychology and Counseling.

Dr. Reynolds has enjoyed a very successful pastoral career serving churches in Arkansas, Missouri, Kansas, and Nebraska. Additionally, he has served as university instructor, consultant, chief parole officer, police chaplain, president of several ministerial organizations, and chairperson of the Federal Fund Review Committee for Health Service, City of Chicago. Other skills include community organizer and leader in local church stewardship development.

Presently Dr. Reynolds serves as pastor of the Centennial United Methodist Church of Kansas City, Missouri. Before coming to Kansas City, he served as pastor of the Gorham United Methodist Church, Chicago, Illinois, 1973-1982, where he led the congregation in a renovation project.

He and his wife, Shirley, live in Kansas City, Missouri and are the parents of three sons.

I would like to preach from 2 Corinthians 3:5 . . . just these words: *our sufficiency is of God.*

You will find that these are the closing words of the 5th verse and it is also my subject. Think with me on these words—Our sufficiency is of God.

I want to go back to the beginning of everything—before there was anything, when there was nothing. God made the world, shaped it—not square, not oblong, not flat, but God made a world and shaped it *round*. Can you?

Then God created every living thing—everything that walks, crawls, flies, swims, that breathes from its nostrils. God put the ore in the earth, flung the stars in the sky, the sun to light up the day and the moon to light up the night. God did it all, made a world and everything in it, above it, and beneath in it. Can you?

Remember the subject is, our sufficiency is of God.

When God had made the world, then God stooped down and formed the world, and created a being. "Then into it he blew the breath of life, and man became a living soul" (James Weldon Johnson, *God's Trombones*).

God started with *nothing* and made a world, made this great, grand and glorious world—and everything in it belongs to God alone. Yes, everything in this world belongs to God; it's God's because God made it. The trees, grass, mountains, rivers, men and women, the ability to think, to talk, to walk, to see, to hear, and the ability to transform that which God has given into other things such as material, energy, and food. To work and use the gifts of life, to sing, to draw, to act and think are all given of God. Yes, the list is endless, all that God has made and allowed us to use and/or transform, comes from our God, who made everything. . . . Our sufficiency is of God.

Life is a precious gift of God, and everything we have is a gift of God. Even the ability to know and appreciate life is a gift of God.

You might ask, Why are we talking about life? Because one of the greatest gifts we have is the gift of life. Related to it is the gift of new life in Christ Jesus. God gives life to us all, and eternal life comes through the gift of salvation from God and Christ Jesus. Our lives are not our own. They have been bought with a price. They belong to God. We are only stewards of life.

The Black church must proclaim today, even more than at any other time in our history, that life is a gift of God and that life belongs to God and that God has allowed us to use this life for a while, for three score and ten. As our foreparent proclaimed long ago, we didn't give it and we can't take it away. Only God can make a life. Neither Black nor White, Red nor Brown can make a life without God.

And I'll tell you this, you will never understand life until you accept Jesus. Yes, nobody knows what life is about until they first know Jesus; if you don't know Jesus, you have no life. You're just walking around day after day . . . groping in the dark, trying to find your way, missing, stumbling, falling, complaining. You know some people can't spend one day of their life without complaining about *everything*. It's either too hot or too cold, too airy or too stuffy. When you know Jesus, you know that what we use for evil, God meant for good. You know that God turns stumbling blocks into stepping stones. Didn't he say it, "I'll make your enemies your foot stool"? Didn't he say I'll make a way out of no way, make a door where there is no door . . . didn't he? . . . didn't he! O yes, you know he did. . . . You know he did, when you know your life belongs to God.

There are two words I want you think on today. The first word is *stewardship*. Luther E. Lovejoy wrote in his book *Stewardship for All of Life*, that stewardship is spiritual and its objective is character. Stewardship is spiritual, and you cannot prove it in the laboratory. Stewardship cannot be proven by reason. Stewardship cannot be proven by scientific investigation. Stewardship is spiritual and to talk about "I don't believe in stewardship," is like saying, "I believe in Christ, but I do not believe in Jesus."

Do you believe your life belongs to God? *Do you* believe Jesus woke you up this morning . . . started you on your way . . . gave you legs to walk with . . . hands to feel with . . . eyes to see with, lips to kiss with? . . . O yes, that's right. Do you mean to tell me that all this just happened? . . . Oh no, I tell you all these are the gifts of God in Christ Jesus. Just the ability to think is a gift of God. You have heard the saying, "A mind is a terrible thing to waste." Young people, get an education, get the B.A. and the M.A. and the Ph.D., and in all your getting remember to get *Jesus*. Get Jesus or all your degrees won't help you in life . . . for *life belongs to God*.

I remember Mrs. Brown, couldn't read or write, but she knew her Bible and knew her Jesus. When the young preacher came to town fresh out of seminary and preached about racism, Black achievements and Black power, Black art, Black music and Black Jesus, Mrs. Brown had said *Amen*, to everything he said except, Black Jesus. When the service was over she said, "Reverend, your show is good, but Jesus is whatever color you want to make him, ain't he?" Yes, Yes, Yes . . . Jesus is white and he's black, he's yellow and he's brown and he's red. He has given life to every person of every color, and no person escapes this Jesus. And you had better believe that the cloak of minority can be no escape from God's love.

One day on the corner of a busy intersection, a young Black man said in the midst of a struggle, "I ain't got nothing to live for. Kill me, I don't care." He didn't know his life belongs to God—and how will people like him know, except you and I go to the streets and houses, highways and hedges, and compel them to come in? Yes there are Black children—hungry, mistreated, lonely—that don't know there's a God. And many of us with our mink coats, diamond rings, Cadillacs, and living where the man just moved out of . . . we ought to remember that it ain't ours, that we need to reach out and tell somebody, that what we have is the gift of God in Christ Jesus and that we are just using it for we are stewards of God. Stewardship, using everything God gave to glorify *him.*

The second word I want you to remember is *existentialism.* It's just a big word to mean *the right-now Christ.* It says I am a steward *right now.* You see, I'm not talking some Jesus way back in Bible days—Jesus that was there for my Mama and my Papa. . . . I'm talking about the *right-now Christ,* the *Jesus today.* I'm talking about knowing this Jesus right now—that I am a steward of *life, right now* . . . *knowing that right now my life belongs to God in Christ Jesus* and that everywhere I go *he* is there.

"If I ascend up into heaven, thou art there: if I make my bed in hell, behold, thou art there. If I take the wings of the morning, and dwell in the uttermost parts of the sea; even there shall thy hand lead me" (Psalm 139:8-10). If I'm sick, lonely, hurt, or just plain feel bad, even there, right there, he is there. God gave us all. Jesus is still giving us, giving to all people everything by grace and divine mercy. This existential Jesus is still healing the sick, still making the lame to walk, and the dumb to talk, the blind to see, and setting the captive free. Glory . . . *glory!* He has loosed my bonds. Great God from Zion, he has loosed my bonds. He has set my soul free. We are free! I've been born anew in his Spirit and washed in his blood.

O one day, one day, we will be called to give an account of our stewardship—an account of our life. Jesus is going to be standing at the gate of the city, with the Book of Life in his hand. He will open it and find your name and my name. And they tell me that we are going to have to give an account of every idle word spoken, every gesture of the hand and every thought. O I tell you, when that time comes I want Jesus to say to God, I know this one, this is my faithful friend. Let him *in. Let them in, glory.* That's when I know our sufficiency is in God, my life belongs to God, when Jesus says, *Come on in, glory.*

I know I'm a steward. One day Jesus will say, "Well done! *I gave to you, and now you gave it all back—your life, your time, your talent, your money, your everything! Everything I gave you, you gave it back to me. Come on up in glory,* for *Jesus, the son of God, holds the power and the decision as to who goes in. And right now, Jesus, right now the joy of life is in your hands. My life is in your hands. My sufficiency is in God.* Amen.

15

GOD'S SOVEREIGNTY

Víctor Bonilla
Puerto Rico

Text: The earth is the Lord's and the fulness thereof, the world and those who dwell therein; for he has founded it upon the seas, and established it upon the rivers (Psalm 24:1-2).

Biographical Sketch

Reverend Víctor L. Bonilla is a native of Puerto Rico. He received the B.A. degree from the University of Puerto Rico, and the Master of Divinity degree from the Puerto Rico Evangelical Theological Seminary.

Mr. Bonilla is a minister who has served as pastor and conference staff person. Presently he is Director of the Conference Council on Ministries and President of the Association of Hispanic Methodist Churches in the Northeastern Jurisdiction.

His experiences in stewardship and evangelism have made him a most valuable resource person in his homeland. Reverend Bonilla is studying for the Doctor of Divinity Degree at McCormick Seminary, Chicago, Illinois. He and his wife, Maria, live in Puerto Rico with their three children.

The best expression of gratitude from a person to God is no other than to recognize God's dominion over all Creation. "The earth is the Lord's and the fulness thereof, the world and those that dwell therein; for he has founded it upon the seas, and established it upon the rivers." When a person recognizes and accepts the truth stated by the writer of the Psalms, an answer of love is given in response to God revealed in Christ Jesus our Lord.

Jesus puts himself under God's will and grace, and serves as a collaborator in the process of giving meaning to the work of our Maker. Jesus is part of that work and discovers all the resources God has given him to serve better, while at the same time he takes responsibility for all living things. We notice that Jesus uses gifts of time, treasures, power, and influence to administer and develop to the fullest his body, mind, and abilities for God's purpose.

In each human being there is an expression of God's love. And we are all one another's keepers. We must be opposed to all exploitation, injustice, dehumanization, that diminish one's dignity and respect. Even though the church is not the only place to begin the relationship with God, nevertheless, it is the holy communion of the redeemed and by all means the best instrument of God to draw persons together.

In order to best understand Christian stewardship, it is essential that we understand some truths we struggle with daily. The greatest of these mysteries is the gospel, the good news that has been committed to our care by God.

It is customary to talk about Christian stewardship in terms of good administration of time, talents, treasures, or any other resource that we understand comes from God. However, none of this would have meaning if we did not enthusiastically and warmly adopt the Great Commission of being messengers of the truth, keepers of the Creation, and good administrators of God's resources in all the land.

I wish to share with you some of the mysteries of stewardship as seen from the persepctive of a Hispanic. Perhaps the greatest of all treasures God has entrusted to us is the gift of life itself.

First I wish to refer to *faith*. As God's stewards we live in a growing and dynamic dialog of divine-human relationships. As we develop our abilities we also, in the same way, develop our capability for faith. It is important to establish the difference between faith and belief. Belief is the way we perceive things in terms of our present knowledge. Faith, on the other hand, is trust in a God who continuously opens life and leads us into unknown avenues. In faith we live beyond ourselves with God's strength.

Thus, as stewards, it is absolutely essential to have an intimate and well-cultivated relationship with God, in order for each moment to have its own value. We move not on the expectation of what is already known but in expectation of what God will reveal to us each day. As the poet said, "Traveler, there is no road; the road is made by walking." We walk with God, who opens greater, more extensive horizons. In moving closer to God, we participate in the fullness of life.

Solely by having faith can we love God with all our hearts, with all our minds, with all our souls, and all our strength. It is only when we move under the direction of God can our hearts, minds, and souls feel completely satisfied.

Faith is the attitude that allows us to hear God's voice, respond to its demands, and utilize to the fullest the gifts of life given to the steward. As we stewards strive to develop all our capabilities to appropriately administer the world that God has placed in our hands, we act out our faith understandings.

Stewardship teaches us that God is continually creating, because creating is God's nature. Because God exists, creation continues. God is revealed through creation. To create is, essentially, to own. Just as a musician expresses himself or herself and the composition he or she interprets is credited to Bach, Beethoven, or Brahms, so it is when God is expressed through Creation. We recognize that "the earth is the Lord's and the fulness thereof, the world, and those who dwell therein." We can determine two things: one, all Creation is an expression of God; and, two, all Creation is complete and unified— that is, no part is isolated from the rest. All creation is related, just as all of the human body is related. It is faith that aids our stewardship understandings.

In other words, stewardship starts from the principle that we live in an orderly world and recognizes that God is revealed in many ways: through nature while worshiping, through the Holy Spirit, through the interrelations in normal human activities. We grow in the knowledge of God when it is revealed in unexpected ways.

Second, let's look at the concept of *grace*, which is directly related to the gift of life and faith. We receive this gift of God's love, not because we deserve it, not on our own initiative, but because God sees fit to give it to us freely. The power and means to live are given to us without interruption. These are gifts from God.

As stewards we recognize that there is a fountain of life, that we are creatures subjected to a relationship with our Creator. If we break away from this relationship we must accept the results, the interruption of our supply of provisions.

Therefore, grace and peace are the manifestations of love from the living God. We can have trust and assurance in the continuous supply of provisions that life requires in order to eliminate anxiety. We find that we have no need to accumulate material things. This way the offering that we give to God will be an extension of God's gifts and a satisfying fulfillment of life, because it is in harmony with the fundamental dynamic of creation. Then the role that a steward plays is not only to be vigilant, but to administer and distribute the gifts of life.

Grace is God's nature. God offers grace to us so that we might participate in life as good stewards. We are stewards of the grace of God, and in no way should we interrupt this process since we will be defeating ourselves. Not to give is the same as isolating ourselves from the grace of God. Our God, the God of Abraham and the God of Jacob, continues to be our Provider. In our greatest expression of fullness toward our Lord, we too must be providers. We cannot participate in grace unless we accept without reservation the presence of God in our lives, thus allowing this presence to be a means of grace for humanity.

When we give, we receive. These are two essential actions for our stewardship. "Silver and gold have I none; but such as I have give I thee," said the Apostle Peter (Acts 3:6, KJV). We can repeat this expression as did Peter and John, as they went up together into the temple which was called beautiful, "From what we have received we will give you." We do not possess more than what God has given us. The person who has received, be it little or much, but who cannot share it with others' lives is an unhappy person.

You cannot use a gift until you receive it, until it is in your hands. You cannot impose a gift. It can only be given. Therefore, to receive is part of our ministry, since it also demands an action of gratefulness. If we are not capable of receiving we cannot give. The result is clear: *when we give we receive and when we receive we give.*

Third, the steward believes that it is more blessed to give than to receive. Giving and receiving are a circular relationship and not like a straight line. As stewards we give because we have received first. To fail to give from what we have received is to stop God's process and flow. Sometimes we believe that a happy life can only be lived when we know we have accumulated great material wealth. We live like the unwise man. We might be thinking that we must destroy our barn since it has become too small. We forget that all of that is waste if we do not have life. This is why someone said, "The dead are not only those in the cold tombs." Many people are "living dead." To give and to receive is the basic rhythm of God's creation. God supplies enough so that we may be generous, and still have enough for our needs.

As stewards we see that someone "takes hold" of our lives. This gives us a sense of "protection and claim of the values" which may be lost. It might also mean an increase in worth for the way we make use of resources. The key word is *use.* There are two definitions for this term. One is to use well until whatever is being used is finished. The other is to use things in such a way that we may always offer something without wearing it out. The latter is the way God uses us.

Let's put it another way: an old piece of furniture is restored and placed so that it may be used. This increases its value. A despised and detroyed human being is redeemed and returns to the place of service with a new value. That way a person is the object of the redeemed love of God. God seeks to make all things anew. Whatever God creates is *good* and what God restores is *good.* That way we are part of God's plan. We can take in our hands what has been damaged and abandoned in order to restore it, compound it, clean it, make a new investment, seek another use of it, and by doing this it is redeemed. For example:

—The lawyer who uses means to unify and restore family ties rather than dissolving them;

—The seamstress who takes the torn dress and mends it so that it looks new;
—The doctor who does not see medicine as a lucrative field, but as the gift of God to restore health, thus restoring life;
—The teacher who frees students from ignorance and provides them with the tools needed in life in order to be led to the roads of wisdom;
—The carpenter who reconstructs the old house and makes it comfortable. God has given us the gift of restoration.

Through all this, stewardship shows us that we should not regard as worthless what God has given. We must remember that the resources of our land are from God. It is our task to understand their proper use, their place, and redeem them so they can be utilized, just as we and our Christian church have been redeemed by the love of God through Jesus Christ. Amen.

A STEWARDSHIP OF SERVICE

Richard Matsushita
Wahiawa, Hawaii

Text: Matthew 25:31-45 — The Judgment.

Biographical Sketch

Richard Tadao Matsushita is a Nisei (second generation Japanese) born in Hawaii. He was raised in a Buddhist home but was converted to Christianity while serving as a chaplain's assistant in the United States Air Force.

He is a graduate of the University of Hawaii and the School of Theology at Claremont, California, where he received a Doctor of Religion degree. Dr. Matsushita holds many honors and religious awards. He is presently pastor of the Wahiawa United Methodist Church in Hawaii, where he has served for several years.

As an Asian-American Christian in Hawaii, I find myself at the crossroads, where the East meets the West. I am a product of that union. An Asian lives in my heart but an American in my mind. How then can an Asian Christian bridge these two cultures and, more important, live out the faith in harmony with both? Let me share my struggles to understand Christian stewardship, as viewed through my Asian-American eyes.

First, what is Christian stewardship?

In Christian tradition the concept of stewardship is central to our understanding of our responsibility to God. A steward is one to whom the responsibility of carrying on Christ's ministry is entrusted. As a member of a local church, a steward pledges to support the ministry of the church with prayers, presents, gifts, and service. Christian stewardship, then, defines all that a follower of Christ is to be and do.

In the Japanese language, however, there is no word for stewardship. The word that comes closest is *hoshi*, meaning service. For Japanese Christians, stewardship means the desire to serve God.

Our scripture reading reflects Jesus' understanding of the stewardship of service. For him service was to be rendered to the needy. The service of compassion to the hungry, the naked, the stranger, the sick, and even the social outcast is the work of the steward. Quiet acts of kindness unknown to others are known to God. Jesus said, "Truly, I say to you, as you did it to one of the least of these my brethren, you did it to me" (Matt. 25:40).

Second, why do we want to serve God?

There is an old story of a man who sat in a dark cave. The only source of light was that which filtered through the cave opening. The man was fascinated by the shadows cast upon the cave wall. The shadows, he believed, were real and represented the totality of life. There was no need to seek further. Contentedly, he watched the shadows dance across the cave wall.

One day, something beckoned him to come out of the cave. He resisted, but finally he gave in to curiosity. He ventured out and, to his amazement, discovered a new world; a world of light, colors, and sound, not just dark shadows on a wall. Never again would he return to darkness.

He who sees the true Light will never return to darkness. Jesus said: "I am the light of the world; he who follows me will not walk in darkness, but will have the light of life" (John 8:12). Once we stood in darkness, but now we see the glory of the Lord.

As Christian stewards we want to serve God because we have been enlightened. We see the new life in Christ.

In the sacrifice of Jesus upon the cross, we see exemplified the full meaning of service. To be in service to God calls us to sacrifice for others. This sacrifice is motivated by Christian love.

Toyohiko Kagawa tells how a Christian missionary helped him to understand the love of God. While he was sick, alone, during his student days, a man knocked at the door. He requested the visitor not to enter, saying: "Do not come in: I have a contagious disease." But the missionary came to Kagawa's side and said, "I have something more contagious than disease. I have come with the love of God" (Charles L. Wallis, *A Treasury of Sermon Illustrations*, p. 145).

This experience left an indelible impression upon the young Kagawa. He went on to dedicate his life to helping others and became an evangelist and a social reformer. He lived among the poor in Japan and served them.

Once when threatened with blindness, he suffered with severe pain in his eyes. During this long period of darkness, he wrote: "Health is gone. Sight is gone. But as I lie forsaken in this dark room, God still gives light. . . . O wonderful words of love! . . . God and every inanimate thing speak to me! . . . Thus, even in darkness,

I feel no sense of loneliness. . . . Prayer continues. . . . In the darkness, I meet God face to face. . . . I am being born, born of God. . . . I am constantly praising God for the joy of the moments lived with him" (Wallis, *Treasury*, p. 145).

As Christian stewards we serve God out of a deep sense of thanksgiving—thanksgiving for God's love that sustains us through the darkest hours.

Finally, what does God ask of us?

In the Gospel of Mark, a scribe asks Jesus, "Which commandment is the first of all?" Jesus answers: ". . . You shall love the Lord your God with all your heart, and with all your soul, and with all your mind, and with all your strength" (Mark 12:28-30). Jesus' commandment is for a total commitment. When we have given our hearts to God, other commitments follow. Service is one form of living out our commitment. What then shall we give?

The Bible establishes the tithe as the measure of our offering to be returned to God. In Leviticus 27:30 it is written: "All the tithe of the land, whether of the seed of the land or of the fruit of the trees, is the Lord's; it is holy to the Lord." The Lord asks a tenth of all that is given to us—and also that the remainder be managed wisely. How, then, will the Christian steward respond? Consider this parable.

"Once upon a time there was a man who had nothing and God gave him ten apples: three apples to eat, three to trade for a shelter from the sun and rain, three to trade for clothing to wear, and one so that he might have something to give back to God to show his gratitude for the other nine. The man ate three apples. He traded three for a shelter from the sun and rain. He traded three for clothing to wear. Then he looked at the tenth apple . . . and it seemed bigger and juicier than the rest. And he reasoned that God had all the other apples in the world . . . so the man ate the tenth apple and gave back to God . . . the core! God has given you enough apples—enough resources and blessings—to supply your needs, plus that with which you may show your gratitude. The choice is yours. Will you return to God the largest and juiciest of your apples, or only the core?" (*Once Upon a Time*, Section on Stewardship leaflet).

To be a steward is to be of service to the Lord and to others. It is the giving of our best to the master in actions and service. What will you give? May it be the good and perfect gift unto God. Amen.

STEWARDSHIP: A CALL TO LIBERATION

Russell F. McReynolds
Flint, Michigan

Text: "The Spirit of the Lord is upon me, because he has anointed me to preach good news to the poor. He has sent me to proclaim release to the captives and recovering of sight to the blind, to set at liberty those who are oppressed, to proclaim the acceptable year of the Lord" (Luke 4:18-19).

Biographical Sketch

Russell F. McReynolds is pastor of Bethel United Methodist Church, Flint, Michigan. He has served the Bethel congregation since 1973. He is a ministerial member of the Detroit Annual Conference. Dr. McReynolds received a Bachelor's degree in Business Administration from Eastern Michigan University in 1970 and the Master of Divinity degree from Gammon Theological Seminary of the Interdenominational Theological Center, Atlanta, Georgia in 1973. His Doctor of Ministry degree was earned in 1982 at the Theological School of Drew University, Madison, New Jersey.

Dr. McReynolds is married to Judy Carol, and they are the parents of four children—Ayana, Malcolm, Caleb, and Nikki. He lives in Flint with his family, where he is very active as pastor, community leader, and servant.

Dr. McReynolds is a Stewardship Associate with the Section on Stewardship, General Board of Discipleship, Nashville, Tennessee.

There is a profound appreciation for freedom in the Black experience in America, and beyond. Our direct experience with physical slavery and overt oppression has brought out of us a desire for liberation more than anything else. We are a transplanted people from the African shores and have not yet made the adjustment to the experience of physical slavery prior to 1864. Laws of discrimination and acts of violence following the passage of the Emancipation Proclamation, policies of institutional and personal racism have blocked every attempt of Blacks to be free since 1864. The dehumanizing effects of second class citizenship call for liberation as the main item on our agenda. The main call of Black America is, "We want to be free."

It is because of the condition of enslavement, physical and mental, and the destructive effects of oppression that the gospel of Jesus is "good news" to us. Black people and others who find themselves enslaved are receptive to the Bible's promise of liberation for all people. Liberation, therefore, is an entrustment, a gift. The response as an oppressed and enslaved people to that entrustment is our stewardship. Stewardship, then, is a call to act on the reality of liberation and freedom as revealed to us by Jesus, the Liberator.

Stewardship and liberation are related best in the Gospel according to Luke, as Jesus declares his own ministry. Luke describes Jesus entering the synagogue on the Sabbath, as was his custom. He stood up to read, and the book of the prophet Isaiah was given to him. He opened the book and found where it was written,

> The Spirit of the Lord is upon me,
> because he has anointed me to preach good news to the poor.
> He has sent me to proclaim release to the captives
> and recovering of sight to the blind,
> to set at liberty those who are oppressed,
> to proclaim the acceptable year of the Lord."
> (Luke 4:18-19)

Members of the Jewish congregation on that day were able to make the association with their condition of oppression and domination; anticipate as a real possibility the expected liberation and liberator; and respond in faith, which was stewardship. They remembered that Moses was called by God to lead the Israelites from Egyptian bondage to the Promised Land, which represented their understanding of liberation. Moses and his people's response to God's call to liberation was their stewardship.

God's intention for freedom, as a second example for Jesus' congregation, is surfaced as they recall the period of exile. The Israelites were dispersed everywhere as part of the conquerors' plan of domination and enslavement. The Israelites were requested to sing the songs of Zion, but they raised a rhetorical question, to reflect a desire for freedom and indicate their stewardship: "How shall we sing the Lord's song in a foreign land?" (Psalm 137:4). They knew freedom was their destiny and therefore acted on the possibilities of that promise, which was stewardship.

Blacks in America, like the Jewish congregation, are able to grasp and appreciate the import of Jesus' declaration of ministry for many reasons. Two have significance: first, Jesus not only read from the Book of Isaiah and announced his ministry, he also *demon-*

strated a ministry of liberation and strewardship through miracles, exorcisms, and healings. It was John's disciples who wanted to know if Jesus was really the Liberator. His response was based on demonstration, which again is stewardship: "Go and tell John what you have seen and heard: the blind receive their sight, the lame walk, lepers are cleansed, and the deaf hear, the dead are raised up, the poor have good news preached to them" (Luke 7:22).

Second, although the prophecy from Isaiah had been read on many occasions, the big difference this time was that the reader himself was the Liberator (or Steward, if you will)—even Jesus, the son of a carpenter, who had grown up in Nazareth. Jesus *was* the content of his announcement.

We as a people are liberated when Jesus becomes the Lord of our lives. Liberation is being in right relationship with God. Our faith response to that right relationship is stewardship, which is our salvation.

As we observe Jesus reading, we notice that this was a shocking and surprising way to declare one's ministry. But that is exactly what Jesus did. He authentically acted out his stewardship in response to the gift of liberation. It was a promise of liberation fulfilled by Jesus who remained obedient and faithful as a steward of an entrustment. That entrustment is liberation.

Jesus is referred to by many titles based on the functions of his person and ministry: teacher, preacher, Savior, the Christ, Son of God, Son of Man, and so on. If we take seriously the pattern of designating Jesus with a title based on function, it is appropriate to call him a Steward in the highest sense of that title. A steward is a person given an entrustment, a trust, and the authority and ability to complete that charge.

Liberation is an entrustment given to Jesus by God to share with all of us. He is a steward, as the Son of God, with all the privileges, rights, and authority of the kingdom of God. He sincerely preached, taught, and shared liberation for the benefit of God and all people.

There are three essential ingredients reflected in the text which emphasize stewardship in realizing God's plan of liberation. First, Jesus as a Steward of liberation was empowered by God's Holy Spirit. "The Spirit of the Lord is upon me." Jesus had to be confirmed and equipped to be a steward. This need is emphasized by acknowledging his second experience with baptism. He received water baptism from John in the river Jordan. As he was coming out of the water, the heavens opened up and the Spirit descended upon him like a dove. God spoke: "Thou art my beloved Son; with thee I am well pleased" (Mark 1:11). Jesus was baptized with the power of God's Spirit. His experience with baptism, both by water and the Spirit, was confirmation of him as a Steward of God. The early church would have this same experience of empowerment at Pentecost. Empowerment by God's Spirit is necessary if we are to be stewards of God's liberation.

Second, "God has anointed me to preach good news to the poor." Anointment is a significant experience in the Old Testament. Kings and prophets were anointed. It was a way of designating a person for special responsibility. The anointing was recognition, designation, and approval by God. Jesus was anointed by God to preach good news to the poor. He was called by God to preach. He was not self-designated, but God-designated. If we are to be faithful stewards of liberation, we must be anointed, designated, and approved by God.

As stewards we are representatives of God and under the authority thereof. We are not under direction of people, but our marching orders come from God. God instructs stewards not to worry about what is to be said. We are to be faithful and obedient. We are anointed to be stewards of liberation. It is for that reason that we as stewards of liberation take the call and anointment of God very seriously.

Third, "He has sent me." As a steward of God's liberation Jesus was sent. He did not come on his own. It is very important, therefore, that we stewards be sent and not come on our own. The sending must be from God. It might mean waiting on God to insure the sending. Many of us find ourselves ready to go, but still we remain in a holding pattern. Patience is necessary. Isaiah is right: "But they who wait for the Lord shall renew their strength, they shall mount up with wings like eagles, they shall run and not be weary, they shall walk and not faint" (40:31). Let the Lord send you if you are to be a steward of God's liberation.

When being sent as stewards of liberation we need to know who the poor are. They are those whom Howard Thurman called "the disinherited and dispossessed" of society *(Jesus and the Disinherited)*. They are the "have-nots" of this world. Their backs are against the wall. They are "the last hired and the first fired." In vain have they put their trust and welfare in corporations, large and small, in governmental programs and politicians, and in other institutions. Jesus, the Liberator, is now their only choice. We are anointed and sent as stewards to preach liberation to persons who are blinded by an inferiority complex, lamed by economic oppression, crippled by political disenfranchisement, and enslaved by racism. We must preach the good news of liberation to those who are indeed "the poor of society."

As God's stewards of liberation—like Jesus, the Steward and Liberator—we are to proclaim release to the victims of racism and oppression. We are to help people recover their sight from self-hatred and low self-regard. We are sent to set at liberty those who are oppressed by institutions and policies meant for their destruction.

We ought not yield to the temptation of underestimating the bigness of God's plan of liberation, yet we must recognize that we are contending against "principalities in high places." We sometimes seem as grasshoppers in the presence of giants. But remember that God can take our resources—material and financial, talents, time and our very selves—and transform them with quickening power into victory and accomplishment. Our faith and trust must be placed in a God who is able.

Finally, our time is now. In Jesus' declaration he proclaimed this as the acceptable year of the Lord. We do not have to speculate and guess any more about the time. *This* is the year of God's favor. Jesus has responded to the call of God. I am sent. Receive me as the Son of God. I am proclaiming this as the acceptable year of the Lord.

There is no doubt, liberation is the thrust of Jesus' ministry. It is God's intention that we be free and not enslaved. God's plan is for us to be in the right relationship, which is a salvation that leads to liberation. This is our destiny. We are not meant to be second class citizens, despised, oppressed, or put down. We are "somebody," because we are children of God moving toward liberation. Jesus was clear about the thrust of liberation. He still offers it to all who will turn to him and repent.

We as stewards of liberation can do no less. We are stewards called, empowered, anointed, and sent to proclaim the liberation that is ours. "Our time under God is now" (*Now Newspaper*, Atlanta, GA). If we are to be faithful and obedient, then we too, like Jesus, must be stewards of liberation, and use all the resources entrusted to us toward that destiny.

GATHER UP THE FRAGMENTS

John Joong Tai Kim
Chadron, Nebraska

Text: John 6:1-14—The Five Thousand Fed.

Biographical Sketch

"John" Joong Tai Kim is a naturalized American citizen born in South Korea. He is a summa cum laude graduate from Methodist Theological College of Seoul, Korea.

Dr. Kim holds the Master of Divinity degree and the Doctor of Theology degree in Pastoral Counseling from Iliff School of Theology, Denver, Colorado.

Dr. Kim began his pastoral experience while a student at Iliff, and was ordained an elder in the Nebraska Annual Conference of The United Methodist Church in 1970. Since that time he has distinguished himself as pastor, conference leader, and Asian Caucus Vice-Chairman of the South Central Jurisdiction. He is also a member of the Council on Ministries of the South Central Jurisdiction and chairman of the Korean American Association of the Jurisdiction. Additionally, he has held the following positions in the conference: Dean of the Pastor's School, Fellowship of Learning, Board of Ordained Ministry Member, and Member of the Committee on the Episcopacy. Dr. Kim is one of the seven elected clergy delegates from his conference to the 1984 South Central Jurisdictional Conference to be held in Lubbock, Texas.

Currently he serves as pastor of The United Methodist Church of Chadron, Nebraska. His services are televised each Sunday, and the church is growing in its outreach and stewardship commitment. Dr. Kim and his wife, Ku Kyun Hahn, are the parents of three children: Rena, Angela, and Emmanuel.

While vacationing in California a few years ago, we took our children to the beach for a swim. The waves which rolled against the beach at regular intervals were challenging, exciting, and invigorating to our children. While we were at the beach, Angela, our second girl, collected a handful of shells, and showed them to me, asking if she could take them home. None of the shells looked special. As a matter of fact, every one of them was a broken piece of shell. The shells she collected were fragments of shells, rather than shells complete and intact. I said to Angela: "Throw them away. They are broken bits and pieces—all fragments. They are no good. You can't take them home. They are not special." Angela reluctantly threw them away.

As I was driving back to our motel, I started thinking. Suppose a child brought a handful of fragments of shells to Jesus at the beach of the Sea of Galilee, asking if she could take them home, what would Jesus have said? Perhaps, Jesus would have said: "Child, take them home with you, and see if you can make use of them. They are precious." On what basis can I make such a conjecture? There was an occasion in which Jesus had something very important to say about fragments. So we returned and picked up the broken shells.

After Jesus had finished feeding 5000 people, he said to the disciples, "Gather up the fragments left over, that nothing may be lost" (John 6:12). He treasured and valued even fragments of food so much that he told the disciples to gather them up. I presume that this command from Jesus to gather up the fragments is a contemporary mandate for all of us to carry out. Yet we do not see any fragments of food here and now. Then, what are the fragments we are supposed to gather up? What exactly *is* a fragment? How do we recognize fragments?

A fragment is a piece which is torn away from the whole to which it belonged. A fragment is a piece which has fallen from a certain level to a lower level, even to the ground sometimes. A fragment is a piece which is far from where it belongs. William Schulz, a modern psychologist, has tried to explain human relationship and its dynamics with only six key terms. These six key relational terms are *in* and *out, top* and *bottom,* and *close* and *far.* If we look at a fragment in light of these six relational terms, we can define a fragment as follows: A fragment is a symbol of those who are *not in, but out, not at the top, but at the bottom, not close, but far.* Thus a fragment may be seen as a symbol of alienation. Whenever we see this relationship in our modern world, we see fragments.

On of our girls, Rena, had a nightmare sometime ago. She and one of her classmates were caught in a snowstorm in open country. There was no other human being to be seen except the two girls in the desolate open country. However, they could see one house in the distance. The girls began to run toward the house for shelter from the snowstorm. Rena's classmate reached the house before Rena. The classmate entered the house, and locked it up. Standing in the cold snowstorm, Rena banged on the door: "Open up! Let me in!" she cried, but her classmate would not let her in.

The dream is a parable of human life. There are storms in the real world of our lives; we experience them daily. For example, there is the storm of disease, the storm of frustration and disappointment, the storm of separation and death. In the dream, the two girls were competing. In the real world we also compete with others. In the dream there was a house, a symbol of the security, affection, acceptance, and approval for which we all strive.

I invite you to take a look at the girl standing outside the house, in the dream, unable to enter. She shows the pain of being left out, the pain of falling behind her competitor, and the pain of being far from the object of her desire and wish. She is a fragment. She represents a vast number of people we call losers, underachievers, or failures. These are the people who are alienated from what they want and need. Every school, every community, and many families have these "fragments" of people. We are called upon to gather them up—to love them, to care for them, to be good stewards of their brokenness.

Let us look at the girl who entered the house. She is certainly a winner. She represents those people we call winners, successes, or achievers. Nevertheless, she is also a "fragment." As long as the storm continues, she will enjoy the shelter. However, when the storm passes, she will not be content cooped up in the house. At this point of her experience, we find a universal problem of human experience, namely we become psychologically alienated from what we have attained. We call this problem boredom or emptiness.

According to an issue of *Time* magazine, Freddie Prinz, after having scaled the pinnacle of success as an actor, said, "Is this all there is? Where is happiness?" He could not find fulfillment in what he attained.

A German proverb describes this universal human problem very well. "When things go well with a donkey, it goes to ice to dance." When the donkey is full and feels good, it wants to do something exciting and dangerous. This proverb is a description of human beings. When we attain what we want, after a brief joy, we don't want it any more. We are like Sisyphus condemned to roll a rock up a mountain only to have it roll down again. Indeed, this problem of emptiness and boredom is a major human problem, especially in affluent countries. This is the testimony of book after book, for example: *Either/Or* by Soren Kierkegaard; *Faust* by Goethe; *The Courage to Be* by Paul Tillich; *The Myth of Sisyphus* by Albert Camus. Thus, even the winners and achievers are "fragments," in that they are psychologically alienated from what they have attained.

May we look at the girl inside the house once more. It is quite possible that she overexerted herself, even hurting herself, when she tried to reach the house before the other girl. If this were true, she represents another category of winners and achievers who have bitten off more than they can chew. Remember Macbeth. He would have been much better off, if he had remained a victorious general. Wanting the throne of King Duncan, Macbeth murdered him. One can hardly describe the severity of agony Macbeth and his wife experienced, after they attained what they wanted. A giant robe hangs loose on a dwarf! A dwarf ought to wear a small robe, not a giant robe. When we try to do and be something beyond our capability, we become alienated from our real selves. Thus we become "fragments."

Therefore, whether we are winners or losers, we are "fragments." This is not all. Sooner or later, we have to die, as all persons must. Do you remember the riddle of how to change a pumpkin into another kind of vegetable? You throw it as high as you can and let it fall to the ground. As the pumpkin hits the ground, it changes into a squash! However, it is a summary of human life! No matter how high one might go up, one has to come down, and end in death— the ultimate fragmentation of life.

If we look at our existence as I have described it in this message, fragment-experience is a universal experience of human life; fragments of humanity are everywhere. This is why Jesus said: "The harvest is plentiful, but the laborers are few" (Matt. 9:37). Jesus calls upon us to gather up the fragments of humanity. It is a part of our stewardship and Christian discipleship.

What, then, are the qualifications of a fragment gatherer (or steward)? Who can be a fragment gatherer? First of all, a fragment gatherer must have a very keen eye. A fragment is rather small, looks insignificant and worthless. It is not likely to catch the eye of ordinary people. Therefore, it takes an extremely keen eye to become a fragment gatherer. You may remember a scene in *The Merchant of Venice* by Shakespeare. Portia has to take for her husband only that man among her suitors who chooses the right casket out of three caskets—gold, silver, and lead. Before Bassanio chooses the lead casket, he makes a sort of speech, looking at the lead casket. One line in his speech I shall never forget: "Thy plainness moves me more than eloquence, and here choose I, joy be the consequences." Neither the brilliance of the gold casket, nor the glitter of the silver casket attracted Bassanio's eye, but the plainness of the lead casket. This says much about the personality and value system of Bassanio. This is the kind of eye a fragment gatherer must have. God calls us to a special type of stewardship that causes us to be intense and enthusiastic in our view and outlook.

A second qualification of a fragment gatherer is to have a hand that's willing to work. The French painter Millet's well-known painting, *The Gleaners,* portrays the kind of hand I am talking about. Fallen ears of grain would not mean much to a rich Nebraskan farmer; but, to poor French peasant women, the fallen ears of grain—even fragments of grain—were so precious and valuable that they took the time to stoop down and pick them up one by one. Likewise, a fragment gatherer of humanity must have that kind of hand.

Whenever I go to a nursing home I cannot but admire the nurses' aides. Their hands are touching hands, soothing hands, guiding hands, lifting hands, feeding hands, and cleansing hands, almost like the hands of Jesus. Their hands are fragment gatherers' hands.

A third qualification of a fragment gatherer is a heightened capacity for being sensitive to others. In the book *If I Perish* by Esther Ahn Kim, we read the autobiographical account of a young Korean Christian who spent several years in Pyung-Yang prisons for her refusal to worship the Japanese Shinto god during the Japanese rule of Korea. Miss Ahn, then, now Mrs. Kim, witnessed to Christian love in a most difficult situation.

The food at the penitentiary was so poor that prisoners actually died of starvation. Some lost their hair. Their vision became dim. Pyung-Yang, capital city of North Korea is as cold in winter as here. There was no heat in the prison cells. In such inhumane circumstances, Miss Ahn demonstrated what Christian love is like. Of so many sacrificial deeds of her love, I would like to mention only one. Miss Ahn volunteered to have an insane Manchurian murderess brought into her cell. This woman could not sleep at night. Her feet would get icy cold. Then, Miss Ahn would bring the Manchurian's cold feet into her bosom and warm them up so that the woman might fall asleep. She demonstrated caring, sensitive stewardship.

A German writer, Karl Zuckmyer, has written an autobiography, and entitled it: *As Though It Were a Part of Me*. Miss Ahn had the capacity to feel the pain and suffering of the murderess as though it were a part of hers. Jesus had that kind of capacity of feeling. How he identified himself with suffering humanity! "When I was hungry, you gave me food. When I was naked, you gave me clothing. When I was in prison, you visited me."

Some of you might say: "I don't have that kind of eye, hand, or feeling you have been talking about. What do I do?" In a small museum near Los Angeles, my family was enjoying beautiful sculptures of marble, bronze, and copper, when I noticed in the midst of these beautiful statues, a broken marble foot, placed rather close to the center of the gallery in a noticeable place. I wondered why in the world a broken foot should be among the masterpieces of sculptures. However, the card placed in front of the broken foot explained that it is a part of a masterpiece of sculpture—a statue of David that had been destroyed by an earthquake. A broken foot in itself would not be valuable, but the fact that it is a part of a masterpiece made it so special that someone brought it to the museum, letting it occupy an immortal place. In Christianity, we have a great affirmation: each of us is a part of the divine: "Everyone is created in the image of God." This is sufficient ground for us to gather up the fragments of humanity.

Moreover, Jesus Christ is the prototype of the fragment gatherer. He gathered up the fragments of humanity, and has instructed us to do likewise. Let us continue in the task of gathering fragments of humanity. What could be nobler than the task and responsibility of a fragment gatherer as stewards of God through Christ our Lord. Amen!

WEEP NO MORE, MY LADY

Jun Ehara
Honolulu, Hawaii

Text: Soon afterward he went to a city called Nain, and his disciples and a great crowd went with him. As he drew near to the gate of the city, behold, a man who had died was being carried out, the only son of his mother, and she was a widow; and a large crowd from the city was with her. And when the Lord saw her, he had compassion on her and said to her, "Do not weep." And he came and touched the bier, and the bearers stood still. And he said, "Young man, I say to you, arise." And the dead man sat up, and began to speak. And he gave him to his mother. Fear seized them all, and they glorified God, saying, "A great prophet has arisen among us!" and "God has visited his people!" And this report concerning him spread through the whole of Judea and all the surrounding country (Luke 7:11-17).

Biographical Sketch

Reverend Jun Ehara, is a Japanese minister who was born in Tsingto City, China. His father served with the Chinese Custom Service (British controlled), and was in diplomatic service of Manchu-Kuo (once existent Manchurian Empire). He spent his childhood in China, Manchuria, Europe, and Japan.

An ordained minister of the Kyodan (the United Church of Christ in Japan), he served as pastor of the Kashima Eiko Church, and Sendai Itsutsubashi Church; and as chairman of the Board of Education, Tohoku Synod, lector of the Tohoku Gakuin University.

When the agreement to send Japanese personnel of the Kyodan to The United Methodist Church in the United States was signed in 1971 between these two bodies, he was chosen as one of two Kyodan pastors to be sent to the United States. He is now a member of the Pacific-Southwest Annual Conference of The United Methodist Church.

Dr. Ehara has served as Japanese Language Pastor at West Los Angeles United Methodist Church (1971-1975) and Harris United Methodist Church, Honolulu (1975-present).

Dr. Ehara received the Master of Theology degree from Tokyo Union Theological Seminary, in 1955; the S.T.M. from Perkins School of Theology, S.M.U., in 1965; and the Doctor of Ministry degree from the School of Theology at Claremont, in 1980. Pres-

ently he is the pastor of Harris United Methodist Church, Honolulu, Hawaii, where he lives with his family.

An Issei mother I knew when I lived in California, had a son named Johnny. He was a very good boy. During the time of World War II, this family had a difficult time, especially when they were in a relocation camp. Just before they were confined in Manzanar, they were in extremely needy circumstances. One day the mother was worrying about what to cook for her son's birthday dinner. At that time Johnny said, "Mom, I like hot dogs. Hot dogs are good. I like them." Of course, he was not saying this because he really liked hot dogs, but, being a thoughtful boy, he was trying to keep his mother from worrying about his birthday dinner.

Shortly after that, the mother, son, and a daughter were confined to the relocation camp in the desert with many other Japanese-American families. Then Johnny, with other young people, volunteered for the army. Leaving his family behind, he went to the European Front. And Johnny never came home—never came home to the relocation camp surrounded by barbed wire, or to their small cottage in San Gabriel Valley, California. He was killed during military action on the European Front. After all these years, whenever Johnny's mother talks about her son, her eyes are always full of tears.

I share this Issei mother's story simply because I want to describe to you the sadness of a widow when she loses her beloved son. In our text from Luke, we see another widow, sad because she lost her only son.

This woman is known as "a widow of Nain." Nain is a town about six miles southeast of Nazareth. She was so sad and was weeping because her only son was dead. Outside the East gate of the town there is a cemetery. According to Jewish custom, a person was buried late in the afternoon of the day of death. Since honoring the dead was supposed to be a meritorious work, a large funeral procession was usually formed.

Jesus happened to pass the gate of the town of Nain with his disciples and many other people. When he saw the funeral and the widow who was in deep grief, his heart was filled with pity for her. He spoke a few words to the widow, translated as, "Don't cry," in the *Good News Bible;* "Weep not," in the *King James Version;* and "Weep no more," in the *New English Bible.*

"Weep no more"—this brief statement contains the deep sympathy and the compassion of the Lord for this woman. In the ancient world where there was no social security or a pension system for the woman, her son was her sole support. The only son was her only hope—but this son was dead. He was gone. What a sad situation, and what a tragedy for her!

Seeing this poor woman, the Lord came over and touched the coffin. Then he said, "Young man! Get up, I tell you!" Then the dead man sat up and began to talk. The Lord gave him back to his mother. The only son of hers who was dead, now was alive. He was lost, but now he was found. This only son of hers was captured by death, but now he was risen!

Observing this incident, people said to one another, "A great prophet appeared among us!"; "God has come to save the people!"

In introducing Jesus in the story, Luke called him "Lord." Jesus is the Lord of life with power over death. He is the master who controls life and death. He is the only master whom we should follow throughout our lives.

Jesus showed deep compassion for the poor, hopeless woman—perhaps because Jesus himself had a widowed mother. Tradition tells us that Joseph was much older than Mary. It is quite natural, therefore, to think that Jesus' mother became a widow when the children were young. This is also indicated in that the Bible tells us nothing about Joseph except in the nativity stories and in the story of Jesus at the Temple when he was twelve. Jesus always befriended widows, orphans, the weak, the poor, and the oppressed.

For those who are in need, for those who are oppressed, for the poor, and for those who are in trouble—compassion is the best remedy. In ancient Greece, when a plague swept over the whole country, many people lost their lives. Thucydides, a famous Greek historian wrote, "It was in those who had recovered from the plague, that the sick and the dying found most compassion."

Compassion heals humankind's diseases. Love cures the sorrow and agony. It is not the material means, but love of heart, that makes people alive in the true sense.

When I went to Russia for a Christian Peace Conference Tour several years ago, I had a chance to visit the famous Moscow bridge. There I was reminded of a very famous story.

Many years ago, when a famine wrought great misery in Russia, the city of Moscow was filled with many beggars, weak and emaciated. Especially in the area around the Moscow bridge there were many beggars. They were all starving and were asking for alms.

The Russian writer Tolstoy was passing by the bridge. Seeing a beggar, he searched his pocket for a coin, but discovered that he had nothing with him, not even a copper piece. Embarrassed,

Tolstoy took the beggar's worn hands in his own and said, "I am sorry, brother. Don't be angry with me. I have nothing with me today." The thin, dirty face of the beggar became illuminated as from some inner light, and he whispered in reply, "But you called me brother—that was a great gift, sir."

Jesus always took the side of the poor, the oppressed, and the forsaken. Our Christian church, from generation to generation, has had deep concern for those people: widows, orphans, helpless and oppressed people. In the Bible we see that great consideration was given to widows. A widow is a biblical metaphor for the helpless ones.

When there was a great famine all over Israel, the prophet Elijah was sent to nobody else but to a woman called Zarephath, who was a widow (Luke 4:26). When a poor widow came to the temple and put two copper coins into the treasury, Jesus said that this poor widow had put in more than all the others who were contributing, for they contributed out of their abundance, but she, out of her poverty, put in everything she had, her whole living (Luke 21:1-3).

In early Christian churches, the first concern that occurred was in regard to widows. According to Acts, there were two language groups in the early church—and there was trouble between them. In Acts 6:1 we read: "Now in these days when the disciples were increasing in number, the Hellenists [Greek-speaking people] murmured against the Hebrews because their widows were neglected in the daily distribution." Therefore, the apostles appointed seven men of good repute, full of the spirit and of wisdom, for the diaconal duties. This is supposed to be the beginning of the order of deacons in the church.

Now, coming back to the text, Jesus, filled with compassion, came over to the sad widow, and gave her son back. What is indispensable for human life is not cold legalism but love. The lookers-on or passers-by could never heal the wound of the widow's heart who was in grief. But the Lord who was full of compassion, could heal the sorrow of her life. As Christians, we have to relate somewhat with the sorrow of the people in need. We must not remain as passers-by.

Several years ago at 5:30 P.M. on a Tuesday, evening rush hour traffic streamed out of downtown Rochester, New York. On the outskirts of the business district, cars and trucks swung onto four-lane Interstate 490 and picked up speed. For most of the drivers, it was the end of another routine day at their offices or plants. Then something happened which made the day different from all other days. As the cars came down on the Route 36 Interchange, a little girl suddenly appeared out of the darkness along the shoulder of the road. She was almost naked, and some witnesses said she was waving as if trying to hail passing cars. They also noticed a car along the shoulder of the road, backing toward the girl.

This was the last time the little girl was seen alive. The police now believe that the drivers saw the last desperate plea for help by Carmen Colon, ten years old, a Puerto Rican girl who had been abducted from her Rochester neighborhood only an hour before. Somehow, police theorize, she momentarily escaped from her abductor in the car on the shoulder of the road in a frantic break for safety. But nobody stopped. Two days later, almost at the same hour of the day, Carmen's body was found in a ditch in a remote section two miles away.

An autopsy showed Carmen had been violently attacked and strangled. The news item closed with this question: "Why did not one of the hundreds of motorists, who passed the girl by, stop to help her? Nobody stopped to help the poor little girl" (Earl C. Willer, *A Treasury of Inspirational Illustrations*). The passers-by probably had no evil intentions: they were not bad people. But they were in a hurry. They had their own homes. They had their own families. They were tired from the day's work and their hot dinner was awaiting them at home. Many people do not want to get "involved."

Remember, Christianity is the religion that has deep concern for others—for the poor, the oppressed, and people in need. Christian churches, from generation to generation, have taken good care of orphans, widows, and the helpless and forsaken. Jesus Christ himself always showed compassion for these kinds of people.

Legalism can never save us—but love can. Christ's new commandment to us is to "love one another." Let us have only love as our commandment. Let us love one another. Especially let us have love and compassion for helpless people, for those in need. Let us be thoughtful of others. Let us be persons of warm hearts. Let us be good stewards of our resources of time and love for others.

Also remember that only the Son of God, who died on the cross, could restore the only son of the widow. This is another biblical metaphor. True sacrificial love for others can achieve the restoration of lost human ties. When our hearts are filled with this kind of love and compassion, then we ourselves can go to the persons who are helpless, in grief, in need. And then we can also say to them, "Weep no more, my lady!"

Thank God—and Amen.

THE STEWARDSHIP OF LIFE'S LEFTOVERS

*Zan Holmes, Jr.
Dallas, Texas*

Text: When they had eaten enough, Jesus said to his disciples, "Collect the pieces that are left over so that nothing is wasted." So they did as he suggested and filled twelve baskets with the broken pieces of the five barley loaves, which were left over after the people had eaten (John 6:12-13, J. B. Phillips).

Biographical Sketch

Zan W. Holmes, Jr. is Associate Professor of Preaching, Perkins School of Theology, Southern Methodist University, Dallas, Texas. In addition to his teaching at Perkins, Dr. Holmes is pastor of St. Luke "Community" United Methodist Church in Dallas.

He served as pastor of Hamilton Park United Methodist Church (1958-1968) before serving two terms in the Texas State Legislature. He then became district superintendent of the Dallas Central District, North Texas Conference, the United Methodist Church before joining the faculty of Perkins.

Educated at Huston-Tillotson College in Austin (B.A. 1956) and Southern Methodist University (B.D. 1959, S.T.M. 1968), Holmes was conferred an honorary Doctor of Divinity degree by Huston-Tillotson. He is active in civic and church life, and is a director of the Dallas Urban League and the North Park National Bank. He was formerly president of the Dallas Pastor's Association and a trustee of S.M.U.

Dr. Holmes was a delegate to the 1972, 1976, 1980, and 1984 General Conferences and a former member of the General Council on Finance and Administration.

He and his wife reside in Dallas where he is chairperson of the North Texas Conference Commission on Religion and Race.

Several weeks ago I attended a district pastors' meeting in Dallas. The purpose of the meeting was to receive an annual stewardship report from each pastor. As I was leaving the meeting, a minister friend said to me by way of a challenging benediction, "Be sure to do your best with what you have left!"

Driving away from that meeting, I kept thinking of those parting words of my colleague, "Be sure to do the best with what you have left." Eventually they led me to recall John's version of the feeding of the multitude.

Jesus was confronted with the hunger of a crowd of people who followed him. In response to the situation, Jesus accepted the generous offering of a lad's lunch of five loaves of bread and two fish, gave thanks to God for it, caused it to multiply, and fed each person in the crowd. After the crowd had finished eating and everyone was filled, there were many pieces of food left over.

Evidently the members of the crowd had ignored the leftovers, because their hunger had been satisfied. The disciples no doubt disregarded the leftovers, because they were celebrating the fact that the demands of the present moment had been met. The lad surely did not notice the leftovers, for he was probably too busy receiving congratulations from those who wanted to commend him for his generosity.

Jesus, however, did not lose sight of the leftovers. In his economy and stewardship, he realized the value of all things. So he said to the disciples, "Collect the pieces that are left over so that nothing is wasted."

It is interesting to note that all four of the Gospel writers— Matthew, Mark, Luke, and John—refer to the food that is left over. It is a significant reference because it highlights the main point of the story—that Jesus is able to supply our needs in abundance. As a matter of fact, more is left over—twelve baskets full—than what was originally offered by the lad!

It is also interesting to note that although all four Gospel writers refer to the *collection* of the leftovers, only in John's Gospel are we given the additional reason: *"So that nothing is wasted."* A stewardship of leftovers is established.

Thus John in his Gospel would have us know that in addition to supplying our needs in abundance, Jesus is concerned about our responsible use of *all* his provisions, including the leftovers! So he says to his modern-day disciples, "Collect the pieces that are left over so that nothing is wasted." Jesus knows that even the leftovers can be used to serve some good purpose in his kingdom.

In the stewardship of life, Black people and other people who have known and continue to know poverty, can readily identify with the words of Jesus concerning the value of leftovers. I suppose that we could write a history of how leftovers have been used to serve some good purpose and meet some great need.

I recall that in the midst of hard times my grandmother used to make many of the clothes she wore. When she finished a garment, there were always a few bits of cloth left over. But she would not throw them away. Instead, in the spirit of Jesus, she would gather them up and use them to make a new quilt or a throw rug for the floor.

When I was a young child, I vividly remember the time when my father used to scrap and save to buy a huge turkey for my mother to cook for our family of eight on Thanksgiving Day. We would eat turkey on the first day, hash on the second day, stew on the third day, and soup on the fourth day—all from that same turkey!

And whenever we had different food items during the week, my mother would never throw away the leftovers. Instead she would place them in the ice box (we didn't know what a refrigerator was!). On Fridays she would put all of the week's leftovers into a big pot and make one big dish. We called each Friday "Leftover Day."

We were grateful for what God had provided and, in the spirit of Jesus, my mother was a good steward of those provisions as she collected the leftovers so that nothing was wasted.

Back in the days of the depression a certain meat-packing corporation managed to stay in business by finding a use for pigtails that had formerly been discarded, and by supplying the market with the hearts and livers of chickens. The milling industry made profits by finding various uses for sawdust. In tight times they learned the value of collecting leftovers so that nothing was lost.

My Black slave forebears learned how to survive the hunger pangs of the cruel system of slavery by finding a use for the leftovers of their day. They took the slave master's discarded food items such as chitterlings, hog maw, pig feet and neckbones, and cooked them in ways that made them edible by their families. As a matter of fact, they were so good at the process that these food items are now considered "delicacies" by many Black people who delight to eat such "soul food" today!

In the spirit of Jesus our slave forebears were making the best of what was left. They collected what their slave masters regarded as waste and used it for survival purposes.

The words of our text and their application by others can have value and meaning for our stewardship of life today.

1. Let us consider the meaning of these words for the stewardship of our natural resources and our relations with others. Who knows—the survival tactics of the poor and the oppressed that made them good stewards of life's leftovers may be the key to the salvation of us all.

We are now beginning to see what the arrogance and greed of the "haves" have done to threaten our capacity to replenish our natural resources, and make life even more miserable for the "have-nots." We are now beginning to see that it is necessary for us to recycle our resources and make use of what was formerly regarded as junk and garbage. We are beginning to see from a "global village" perspective that we must truly learn to "live simply if others are simply to live."

We must now begin to see the urgency of the warning of the late Dr. Martin Luther King, Jr., who said, "Either we learn to live together as brothers and sisters or we perish separately as fools."

But when Jesus said, "Collect the pieces that are left over so that nothing is wasted," he also challenged other areas of our lives.

2. In the *stewardship of our talents, resources, and abilities* his words challenge us to concentrate upon the use of what we have left instead of concentrating upon what we do not have.

One of the tragedies of life is the amount of time we waste dreaming about all the things we would do if we had the necessary money, ability, or power. We *dream* about doing *great* things for others, but seldom do we *wake up* and use what little resources we do have available. Carlyle once said: "It would be better for a person to actually build a *dog house* than to spend his time dreaming about the erection of a palace."

Too many of us are like the one-talent man Jesus discussed in the parable of the talents. Two others were given more talents than he. As a result, he was so worried over the fact that he had fewer talents that he would not even risk using his one talent. So he buried his talent in the ground. I often think of people I've known during my ministry who have excused themselves from doing God's word by appealing to what they do not have. "I'm too old." "I'm too young." "I'm not educated." "I'm not experienced." "I'm not the right color." "I'm not good enough."

But Jesus is not concerned with what we do not have. Instead he says, "Collect the pieces that are left over so that nothing is lost." In other words, "Do the best you can with what you have left."

> It's not what we'd do with a million
> If riches should be our lot.
> It's what we're doing now
> With the dollar and quarter we've got.
>
> —Anonymous

When God asked Moses to go tell Pharaoh to let the children of Israel go, Moses began to complain about what he did not have. He said, "Who am I that I should go. . . . I am not eloquent. . . . Behold, they will not believe me." After listening to Moses' complaints, God said to him: "What is that in thine hand?" In other words, God was saying, "Moses, I'm not interested in what you do not have; I'm only interested in what you have. . . . Stretch forth thine hand . . . and certainly I will be with thee."

Yes, in the *stewardship of our talents, resources, and abilities* God wants us to do the best we can with what we have left.

3. When Jesus says, "Collect the pieces that are left over so that nothing is wasted," he also challenges us to be *faithful stewards of our wounds.*

Tragedy is sure to come into every life. There will be times when we will suffer losses. But even in such times our text reminds us that Jesus would have us concentrate upon what's left instead of concentrating upon what's gone. For somehow, through the grace of God, resources are left to carry on.

I was sharply reminded of this sometime ago as I read a local newspaper. There on the front page was the picture of a young and beautiful Black mother born without arms and legs. The State Department of Public Welfare had charged in court that she was incapable of taking care of her five-month-old daughter.

During the court hearing the mother surprised everyone by proving she was competent to take care of her baby. There before their eyes she undressed and then dressed the baby again by using only her lips and tongue. The judge was so impressed that he not only awarded custody of the baby to her, but said, "I have to commend you very much for your courage, spirit, and ingenuity. . . . You have proven that physical endowments are only a part of the spectrum of resources that human beings possess. . . ."

This young Black mother was a good steward of her wounds. Rather than dwell on what she did not have, she chose to collect the broken pieces of her life that were left and do the best she could.

As oppressed minorities in a society which has a history of dehumanizing us, both physically and spiritually, those of us who are both Black and Christian can affirm that in spite of the circumstances of our life God has endowed us with courage, spirit, and ingenuity through Jesus Christ our Liberator.

For example, the gift of the Negro spirituals testifies to the fact that the Black slaves were faithful stewards, even of their wounds. They refused to waste their suffering. Instead, they used it to deepen their faith. Even though they sang, "Over my head I hear trouble in the air," they also sang, in the same song, "There must be a God somewhere."

Thus, in their suffering, they did not despair before Jeremiah's question when he asked, "Is there no balm in Gilead?" (Jeremiah 8:22). Instead, they straightened out the crook in the question mark and made it an exclamation point! As good stewards of their wounds they shouted the Affirmation of Faith: "There is a balm in Gilead to make the wounded whole!"

It is their gift of this affirmation that encourages us as faithful stewards to do the best with what we've got left! Thus they join Jesus as he says to us, "Collect the pieces that are left over so that nothing is wasted." Indeed, use *everything* to the glory of God! Amen.

SUCH AS I HAVE

Mary Lou Santillán Baert
Nashville, Tennessee

Text: "Silver and gold have I none; but such as I have give I thee: In the name of Jesus Christ of Nazareth rise up and walk" (Acts 3:6, KJV).

Biographical Sketch

Mary Lou Santillán Baert is a native Texan, and the second child of eleven born to her Mexican parents. She holds the B.A. degree from Southern Methodist University of Dallas; a Master of Art degree in Christian Education from Scarritt College of Nashville, Tennessee; a Master of Art degree in Journalism from Syracuse University, New York; and a Master of Theology degree from Perkins School of Theology (SMU) of Dallas.

Ms. Baert taught school in Texas, served fourteen years as a missionary in Mexico, and has given many hours as a Red Cross volunteer. She also served as a volunteer in Germany and other locations in Europe and the USA.

Ms. Baert and her husband Simon are the parents of two sons, Timothy and Reimund. She has received many awards and honors, including three from Perkins Seminary, one of which was in the field of voluntary activity in support of social causes.

She speaks, reads, and writes Spanish fluently. Before assuming her present position as coordinator for ethnic minority resource development with the Curriculum Resources Committee, Board of Discipleship, Nashville, she served as pastor of churches in Port Arthur and Dallas, Texas, and Great Britain.

In the setting of our text, Peter and John are the main actors. It was the hour of prayer. They were on their way to the temple to pray. At the gate of the temple a lame man—lame from birth—had been carried to sit and beg from those who entered. He had been brought there daily for over forty years.

As Peter and John were about to enter the temple, the lame man asked them for alms. What could they give? They were not rich or prosperous. Their future was not that promising. How easy it would have been to smile and say, "Sorry, but we are poor ourselves and we have nothing. God bless you," and then to have gone in to say their prayers.

But instead they stopped. Peter fastened his eyes on the lame man and said, "Look at us." And the man looked at Peter and John, probably expecting to receive something, anything, a coin or two. How he must have longed for something good to compensate for his sad and miserable life.

Peter said to the lame man, "I have no silver or gold, but I will give you what I do have. In the name of Jesus Christ of Nazareth, walk." And Peter took the lame man by the right hand and lifted him up. The lame man's feet and ankles became strong, and he not only walked, but he leaped and entered the temple and praised God! All who saw him, certainly those who had known him for so many years or had carried him, were astonished and were filled with wonder and amazement.

Neither silver nor gold, but such as they had, they gave. That is stewardship. Sharing that which we have is our proper stewardship.

Peter and John responded to the needs of the lame man with what they had. They used the gifts God had given them—not what belonged to others or excuses for what they did not have, but such as they had, they gave.

Stewardship is more than recognizing what we have. Stewardship rests on the response we make. Stewardship begins with the commitment of our life. Before the churches in Macedonia begged for the favor of taking part in the relief of the saints and before they gave sacrificially, they "first gave themselves to the Lord." It is the love of God in us that allows us to share our gifts in response to so great a love.

We can give *our* time, *our* talent, *our* money, *our* prayers, *our* service, and it becomes *our* mediocre offering to God simply because we claim it as *ours* and give it with strings attached. It costs us nothing, and the tragic thing is that we are content.

A story of King David in the Old Testament is a good example of how we must offer our best to God in all things. David took the census of his people, and the Lord became angry. But God allowed him to choose his own punishment: seven years of famine, three months of fleeing from his enemies, or three days of pestilence. David chose the pestilence because he felt it was better to fall into the hands of God than humankind. The pestilence came and thousands died. Just as the angel of death was about to strike Jerusalem, God put a stop to it. David, on seeing the destruction, asked God to punish him alone, for it was he who had done wrong and he pleaded with God to save his people.

The prophet Gad came to David with a message from God: "Build an altar on Araunah's threshing floor to God." So David went to build the altar. When Araunah saw David coming, he went out to meet the king and asked him why he had come. David explained that he had come to buy his threshing floor to build an altar to the Lord so that the plague which had attacked the people might be stopped.

Araunah offered everything to the king with no strings attached, oxen and all. David could have been flattered at such generosity, but instead he replied, "No, I will buy it from you; I will not offer to the Lord my God whole-offerings that have cost me nothing." So David paid the price and built the altar and offered a sacrifice. And the plague stopped. God was worthy of a sacrifice and David thus offered it.

Stewardship means giving ourselves freely to the Lord so that the kingdom may enter our hearts. If it does not enter there, it will never come. When we belong to the kingdom of heaven, then everything we have belongs to God. Perhaps that is one reason we are asked a very important question when we join the church: "Will you be loyal to The United Methodist Church, and uphold it by your prayers, your presence, your gifts, and your service?" When we answer such a question, we give account of our stewardship before God and before the church. Have we said "yes" out of commitment or just to answer an embarrassing question quickly?

"Such as I have"—time to pray, time to sustain a strong relationship with God, time to utter our heart's sincere desire and that of others, time to listen to God's will.

"Such as I have"—time to gather with others to worship God. The pastor is expected to be in the pulpit every Sunday. And the congregation?

"Such as I have"—freely we have received, let us freely give. Gifts, great or small, offered to the Lord become a blessing to us and to others. We often fail to give because we fear God will make extraordinary and exorbitant demands of us or that God will take away all that we have, all that we have earned with our sweat and efforts, and that we will be left with nothing. And yet we stand up in church and proclaim and confess that God is love. How can we fear such a God of love?

"Such as I have"—talent and ability to serve. We talk, yea, even preach, about the church being the servant arm of the Lord, and we make no commitment. We hold back our lives, our talent, our possessions, our heart. We need to look not only at the needs of the world, but also at what God has entrusted to us. We tend to separate the two. God's purpose for us is to share what we have—nothing more, nothing less, but such as we have. We must want for others what we desire for ourselves.

I grew up in the midst of a poor people, a rejected people, an alienated people. It was very hard for many of the families to live in that Dallas community. The Mexican parents would take their children out of school and go where the crops were being harvested in order to have work. Children and youth and adults would work so that the family could survive. Many times the teachers would ask the families who migrated to leave at least one child behind to get an education so he or she could make it in life. But none of the Mexican families would accept such an idea. It was not a matter of one surviving, but of all surviving. What was good for one, must be good for all. Were not all worthy?

Stewardship is living, working, and giving in order that good may come to all, not just to one or a few. Justice is a part of our stewardship.

Today we are an affluent church. We have the silver and the gold, but not the power to say "rise up and walk!" We have prided ourselves in our intelligence, we have rejoiced at our ability to invest and prosper at the expense of others' labor and health, we have celebrated our lack of want and we have prayed that we will never be poor.

Being good stewards, God's stewards, implies several things. For example, it means accepting responsibility for fulfilling God's will by allowing God to make claims on us and on the gifts God has entrusted to us. It means accepting this obligation of stewardship with faithfulness—not when we feel like it or want to ask a favor of God.

It means joining with the other members of Christ's Body to do what one person alone cannot do.

It means witnessing to God's kingdom within us that Shalom may come.

It means glorifying God with one's life and gifts.

It means emptying ourselves and taking the form of a servant.

It means serving God and others with all our heart, with all our soul, with all our strength, with all our mind, and with all our love.

It means looking and seeing the lame people at our doorsteps, calling them brothers and sisters, offering them a word of hope, and responding to their need.

It means offering ourselves with prayer and love, and such as we have to God, that the Word who became flesh may continue to walk and dwell among us, bringing wholeness to all.

Come, then, such as you are and offer it all to God—such as you have, nothing more and nothing less . . . and surrender it to God.

BLESSINGS THAT COME THROUGH SHORTAGES

Edward E. Bufford
New York, New York

Text: When Jesus then lifted up his eyes, and saw a great company come unto him, he saith unto Philip, Whence shall we buy bread, that these may eat? And this he said to prove him: for he himself knew what he would do. Philip answered him, Two hundred pennyworth of bread is not sufficient for them, that every one of them may take a little. One of his disciples, Andrew, Simon Peter's brother, said unto him, There is a lad here, which hath five barley loaves, and two small fishes: but what are they among so many? (John 6:5-9, KJV).

Biographical Sketch

Edward Eugene Bufford is a native of Birmingham, Alabama. He is a graduate of Miles College of Birmingham, receiving the B.A. degree, and Gammon Theological Seminary of Atlanta, Georgia, receiving in 1973 the Master of Divinity degree.

Dr. Bufford has been awarded the D.D. degree from the Theological Seminary of Birmingham, along with many other honors, awards, and special recognitions.

He has pastored churches in Alabama, California, and Tennessee. Before accepting his present appointment, he served for seven years as director of evangelism with the General Board of Discipleship, The United Methodist Church in Nashville, Tennessee.

Dr. Bufford is active in community affairs, and a member of Alpha Phi Alpha Fraternity, Inc. Presently he is pastor of Brooks Memorial United Methodist Church of Long Island, New York. He and his wife Joycelyn are the parents of one daughter.

The text for our message is taken from John's account of Jesus' great miracle of the feeding of the five thousand—an account quite familiar to most of us.

The miracle is probably not one of the most astonishing or acclaimed of Jesus' miracles. It, however, provides us with a great lesson of stewardship for today and all times—a lesson that teaches us to use wisely that which we have, while trusting God to bless us in our shortages.

Authorities are uncertain of the exact location in which this moving experience takes place. It is safe, however, to say that Jesus was somewhere near the province of Galilee—preaching and teaching—doing God's will.

Let us look more closely into this account.

Jesus had departed from the seashore of Galilee where hundreds and perhaps thousands had gathered to hear him speak words of wisdom and truth! Men, women, and children stood in awesome wonder, and were lifted from the routine of common ordinary experiences to the breathtaking heights of divine spiritual encounter.

I do not pretend to know all that Jesus said to the people on that day. Neither do I know what they said about him. I do know, however, that Jesus made such an inspiring impression upon the people that they followed him, and listened to his words.

As we enter the story, we see Jesus out in the deserted, barren, desolate place. After he has preached what must have been a marvelous sermon, after he has answered their most profound and probing questions about God and the kingdom—the scripture says that the people became hungry!

The setting is clear: after they had heard his words of comfort and inspiration, witnessed to his act of love and kindness, seen his ability to heal the sick and restore feeble bodies—they still needed something else. The record says they needed physical food to satisfy their hunger. Say what you will, when mealtime comes, nothing will satisfy our physical need for nourishment but food. As Maslow says, until our most basic needs of food and shelter are satisfied, it is hard for us to function.

Jesus understood this fact—*so much so that when he received word* that those who had followed him into the desert were hungry, it disturbed him. It disturbed him so much that he called an emergency meeting with his disciples and instructed them to survey the crowd and look among the people to see what was available.

The disciples returned with a negative report. Like many of our boards or committees, their report sounded discouraging. They reported sadly, Lord we have "a shortage."

We have "checked our treasury" and can only find 200 pennies! We looked among the people and in the crowd and there is only one person who brought a lunch, a little boy who has five loaves of bread and two small fish—but that too is insufficient!

They said to Jesus, send the crowd away, for we have a shortage. All we have is enough for ourselves, not 5,000 others.

Jesus listened to their report, and when they had finished talking about the "shortage," he said, "Now wait just a minute. I can't send these people away! The only problem that we have is that *you have gotten mixed up on your arithmetic,* and your accounting procedure is turned around! Your math is out of whack. You counted the pennies, you counted the bread, you counted the fish, and added up the people. *But you didn't count me!"*

Whenever we count what we have, or don't have, and fail to count Jesus, that's bad arithmetic! Any time we look over our situation and fail to include Jesus, we help to construct our own system of failure and disappointment. Whenever there is not enough to meet the need, whenever the situation becomes crucial, whenever there is a shortage—don't forget to call on Jesus, God's only Son. He promises to supply our greatest needs.

As we recall our text, we discover that this was not only unique in that day, because shortages also occur in our day and time. For example:

1. Many churches are straining and struggling to keep their heads above water—struggling just to survive. As a result, the faithful few must stand together and try to make it—in spite of the shortage.
2. Many homes are experiencing serious financial and spiritual troubles—coming apart at the seams because there is a shortage of love and commitment within the family.
3. Our bodies also suffer shortages. There was a time when some of us walked with steps that were swift and graceful, and now we find that we have to take one slow step at a time. This is a physical shortage.
4. Then there are other shortages in life, such as psychological, sociological, and anthropological. Shortages are all around— and if you haven't experienced them yet—just keep living. Shortages are a part of life.

No one wants a shortage. Shortages are not welcomed. But the fact is, there are some "blessings," some good things, some positive values that come through shortages. For example:

1. Shortages will keep us humble. They keep our heads from becoming too big. Haven't you noticed that when some folks get everything they need, you can't tell them anything. But when they don't have much, they become very humble and kind.
2. Another blessing that comes through shortage is that shortages will keep us closer to God. A shortage will make us bow down on praying knees. Oh, yes!

3. And last, shortages give us the opportunity to see the power of God in action in our lives.

Because of the shortage of food in the story of our text, Jesus was able to teach the disciples that with God all things are possible through faith!

Can't you see him as he instructed the crowd to sit down. He told the disciples to bring the 200 pennies—the loaves and the fish—and place them in his hands.

Then he said, "In your hands it *looks small*, but in my hands it becomes *large*. In your hands it looks like *defeat* but in my hands it becomes *victory*. In your hands it looks like weakness but in my hands it becomes *strength*. In your hand it looks like *despair*. In my hands it *becomes hope*. What you consider a shortage is often God's opportunity to shower us with blessings."

Jesus took the loaves and two fish, and fed the 5,000 hungry souls, and there was some left over.

It always works that way. When we step out on faith and give God what we have, God will bless it and give us the victory. The stewardship of shortages is to use wisely all that one has, no matter how little or how much. Whenever we turn it over to God through Christ Jesus our Lord, a blessing takes place.

It was true with Moses, in Egypt, as God instructed him to go to Pharaoh and to use what he had to gain freedom for his people Israel. Moses used what he had and was victorious.

It was true of Daniel, when put in the lions' den. He used what he had available to him . . . prayer and faith in the Almighty God. He, therefore, prayed and was delivered. God sent an angel to free him from the lions' den. His blessing came in spite of the shortage.

It will be true in your life, if you but give your life to God as a steward of God's grace, love, and mercy. Will you give yourself totally to God as a faithful steward today?

Your shortages will be God's opportunities to work miracles in your life and the life of your loved ones. Stewardship is committing our shortages to God our Creator, and Jesus our Lord. To be a good steward means to trust God in all things, and manage to the best of our ability whatever we have, regardless of how small or large. God knows our every need, and will surely supply all of our needs through grace. Amen.

WHAT TO DO (AND NOT DO) WHEN IN FINANCIAL TROUBLE

Roberto Escamilla
San Antonio, Texas

Text: Luke 16:1-13—Parable of the Unrighteous Steward.

Biographical Sketch

Roberto Escamilla is a native of San Antonio, Texas. He has served as Associate General Secretary for the Division of Evangelism, Worship and Stewardship of the Board of Discipleship. Dr. Escamilla is recognized widely as a leader in these areas of ministry. He is the author of several books, including *A Feast of Life* and *Prisoners of Hope*, which is published both in English and Spanish, by the Upper Room.

Presently he is the pastor of Los Angeles United Methodist Church of San Antonio, Texas, where he resides with his wife Dorothy and children.

There is hardly anyone who has not at one time or another found himself or herself in some kind of financial bind. In these days of high inflation, it is common for persons to overspend and strain their budgets. Our salaries rarely keep up with the rate of inflation. Many of us are tempted to give in to all kinds of "bargains" and "special sales," and we oftentimes end up buying "stuff" that we don't really need in order to make ends meet. There is always a tendency to say, "Just charge it!" Or we pull out the all-familiar credit card and sign. Thirty days later, when the bills arrive, we panic! Our spending causes us to get deeper and deeper in debt. What do we do, or not do, when financial trouble comes our way?

The first tendency is to rely on friends or relatives. Sometimes they can come to our rescue. More often than not, this could be an abuse of friendship or kinship, and a rather embarrassing procedure. Friends and relatives mean to be helpful, but there is the risk of overloading them—to wear out our welcome! After all, they also have their own bills to pay, and ultimately no one wishes to be obligated to help or be indebted to any other person. So, what do we do? The second tendency is take out a loan. However, this only puts us deeper and deeper in debt.

In the New Testament there is an interesting story with a contemporary flair. It is about a man who found himself out of a job and, therefore, in financial distress. While he still had some authority, he decided to decrease the amounts that his clients owed the company in order to befriend them so that when he needed their help they would be obligated to provide a place for him to stay. It was a clever device! He was an astute man! As a matter of fact, he was commended for being so clever. But on the other hand, needless to say, this was an irresponsible and foolish way to secure his own future.

This is what not to do when in financial trouble—that is, to attempt to manipulate others in order to reap the benefit of their indebtedness. It is a dishonest device. He did not "own" the company, and his responsibility was only to be a steward. In this example he was a poor steward at that! His intention to gain the favor of his subordinates was not the thing to do!

In concrete terms, if a person is in financial trouble, he or she is not to:

- Turn to friends for rescue;
- Keep on buying and getting further and further into debt;
- Get a new loan to pay for all of the other loans (unless it is at a lower interest rate!);
- Panic and despair and feel that all is lost.

All these things are expressions of poor stewardship. They are the things not to do. They will bring despair and trouble.

On the other hand, there are some very specific things we can do when in financial trouble.

First, we can use what we have wisely. As a matter of fact, it is possible to utilize what we have in such a way as to make a significant difference in the world for the good of others and ourselves. All that we have is a trust from God placed in our hands to manage and share with others. God expects us to be responsible managers and utilize wisdom in the administration of our finances and other resources. We are held accountable for our stewardship in the context of eternal values.

What to do, then, when in financial trouble? I would suggest that we are to demonstrate our responsibility on a broad scale. That is, even with limited financial means we are to be as accountable as we can, to practice restraint. "The person who can be trusted in little things can also be trusted in great" (Luke 16:10, paraphrase).

Walter Rauschenbush hoped that "when our use of this world is over and we make room for others, may we not leave anything ravished by our greed or spoiled by our ignorance, but may we hand on our common heritage fairer and sweeter through our use of it." We, as stewards, have a responsibility to shape, not only our own destiny, but the destinies of the world. We have the power to fight against injustice and poverty, and hunger, and anything that dehumanizes. Especially do we have the power to dream, to have a vision of a better world.

Second, it is important to recognize the extraordinary significance of small things. We must begin where we are—even in financial trouble, or in poverty, or with scant resources. The modern-day definition of success is normally related to "bigness." We normally think of large corporations and impressive statistical reports when we think of success. The greater the sales, the greater the success and impact. This is important in a highly secularized culture and from a secular perspective, but one needs to be reminded again and again of the precarious nature of success in biblical understandings. There is such a thing as the "crisis of promotion," the success of faithfulness unto God.

On the other hand the extraordinary significance of little things, of small beginnings, points out that it does not matter how much money or how many talents we may have, what does matter is how they are invested, how they are used, how they are multiplied and scattered about like seeds in fertile soil. Frequently minorities and poor persons get discouraged, feeling that they don't have much to contribute in the way of material possessions or talents to the church and world. But the hidden resources—invisible, intangible, though small—may frequently turn out to be decisive in the life of our world. There is always the *one* talent that must be utilized if it is to be increased. The criterion, it seems to me, is not the size of the accomplishment, but the willingness to be faithful and responsible here and now with what we have.

Persons with limited economic resources have difficulties when the monthly bills come and they are unable to take care of all of them. They find themselves under tremendous pressures. However, that which gives us stability and enables us to be responsible stewards is found in the concept of *hope*. Hope, based not upon the shaky circumstances of life, nor on the environment in which we live, but hope in the God who owns the whole earth and has made us managers, stewards of all creation. "Why do you spend your money for that which is not bread, and your labor for that which does not satisfy?" (Isa. 55:2, RSV).

These are indeed days of anxiety, fear, and frustration, particularly in relation to a "shaky" economy. What to do when in financial trouble? Move forward with hope in a God who does not abandon, who is able to empower us to achieve greater things in a world of expanding horizons.

We must rediscover the potential of "small things" and find ways to invest in such a way as to receive the dividends of God's insurance for our life. This is the "fine print" which spells out a victorious spirit, a spirit that transforms small and seemingly insignificant things into greater and more significant accomplishments. We must identify and participate in God's activity precisely in and through the small things.

It was Churchill who stood up in Parliament and said bluntly, "It is not the time for persons who have political work to do, to dream easy dreams of brave new worlds." The challenge of shaping a newer world is forever before us. There is always the possibility of beginning now and moving forward, and in so doing initiate the process whereby something that was apparently small gathers momentum and makes a significant difference.

Third, sound stewardship principles emerge out of recognition that *God alone is our God* and is in charge. We live in a time when there seem to be many "other gods." We can find wholeness as we are willing to recognize the idols—the other gods, and identify them as gods with feet of clay which knowingly or inadvertently we worship daily. God is calling us anew to examine our loyalties and to rearrange our priorities. Total allegiance to God alone is the basic prerequisite for true discipleship. "No servant can serve two masters; for either he will hate the one and love the other, or he will be devoted to the one and despise the other. You cannot serve God and mammon" (Luke 16:13). The problem as stated is that the love of "things" lowers our sights so that we focus on the creature and not the Creator. This attitude has always been identified theologically as elemental sin.

The thing to do when in financial trouble is to examine our values. There is a sense of ambiguity prevalent in our time. There are pressures and demands placed upon us every day. These things are all important, but what is really essential?

To worship one God and not two (God and mammon) is the center upon which we build our lives, recognizing the one God who alone gives real meaning to our existence. It means that we shall endeavor to cease giving second-rate causes our first-rate loyalties. It implies that we will not allow gold and silver bathroom fixtures to become the criteria for status for a successful or significant life.

I believe there is a kind of atheism in our time when, on the one hand, we affirm a positive belief in God as revealed in Jesus Christ, and then live as if God did not exist. This creates a spiritual vacuum which opens the door to all other idols, which eventually leads us to financial trouble.

An interesting exercise would be to simply list on a sheet of paper the things that mean most to you in life. I am sure you will include your family, job, house, church, friends, money, etc. Then enter into a process of doing an honest ranking of priorities. I wonder what

place you would ascribe to God on your list, and to the church.
John Wesley gave us an excellent definition of an idol when he identified it as "whatever takes our heart from God . . . whatever we see happiness in, independent of God."

It is possible to allow the subtleties and self-deception of idols to grasp us and keep us in bondage. Sometimes they come disguised as chromium-plated objects or some other enticing appearance of American ingenuity. The tragic results are always a disaster of bitterness and disillusionment when we place our total trust in these things. There comes a time in our lives when we turn from all other lesser loves to the one and only God who alone determines our destiny.

The thing to avoid when in financial trouble is to pursue the same lifestyle of the past, ignoring our debts and hoping they will disappear. The thing *not to do* when in financial trouble is to evade the issue of the inadequacy of temporal remedies to our situation. The thing *to do* is to discover new resources and new possibilities hidden within us that will bring about a total reorientation of our priorities and to focus our attention upon life's enduring values. Something needs to happen in order to enable us to change our basic pattern.

This is the day that God has given you to decide how you would envision your life in relation to your gifts, both material and spiritual. Would you do an inventory of where you are? If you find disloyalty or are mastered by extreme ambition or greed, would you be willing to rearrange your priorities?

COSTLY GIVING

Joseph B. Bethea
Raleigh, North Carolina

Text: And he sat down opposite the treasury, and watched the multitude putting money into the treasury. Many rich people put in large sums. And a poor widow came, and put in two copper coins, which make a penny. And he called his disciples to him, and said to them, "Truly, I say to you, this poor widow has put in more than all those who are contributing to the treasury. For they all contributed out of their abundance; but she out of her poverty has put in everything she had, her whole living" (Mark 12:41-44).

Biographical Sketch

Joseph B. Bethea is a native of Dillon, South Carolina, and the son of a Methodist minister. He holds the B.A. degree from Claflin College, Orangeburg, South Carolina; the Master of Divinity from Gammon Theological Seminary, Atlanta, Georgia: and has done advance study at Union Theological Seminary, Richmond, Virginia. In 1974 he was awarded the Doctor of Divinity degree from Gammon Theological Seminary of Atlanta.

Dr. Bethea has served seven pastorates in South Carolina, North Carolina, and Virginia. He has distinguished himself as a Lecturer in Preaching at Duke Divinity School and at many annual conferences across the U.S.A. Dr. Bethea has published several articles, including Methodism Alive in North Carolina *(1976)*. He has been General Conference delegate five times, and led his delegation in 1984.

Before being appointed to his present position as Administrative Assistant to the Bishop and Coordinator of Ministerial Relations, North Carolina Conference, he served for six years as District Superintendent of the Rockingham District, North Carolina Conference.

Dr. Bethea, his wife, and daughter reside in Raleigh, North Carolina.

It was time for the presentation of tithes and offerings at the temple in Jerusalem. It was the Passover season, and the faithful had gathered from throughout the kingdom to remember and celebrate God's deliverance of the children of Israel from Egyptian bondage. They were participating in one expression of their loyalty to the religion of their fathers. They were putting their money into the treasury. This act was only one expression of their loyalty, for any adequate concept of stewardship must also include the giving of our time, our abilities, and ourselves, as well as our money.

God does not expect all of us to do everything in the church. However, God expects all of us to do something in and through the church. Some can teach church school classes, or lead groups of children, youth, and adults. Some can sing in choirs or serve on boards, councils, commissions, or committees. Some can serve in the outreach ministries of the church or at connectional levels of the denomination, or on civic or community boards or task forces. All cannot do everything, but each can do something; and every true child of God is anxious to share a portion of time, abilities, and self in the work of the Lord and the mission of Christ's church.

In the text, Mark 12:41-44, Jesus is calling specific attention to the obligation of the loyal to give money to the work of the Lord. Multitudes were moving about the temple on this occasion, putting money into the treasury, and Jesus sat nearby to watch. He noticed the well-to-do contributing large sums, and surely Jesus was pleased with the gifts that came out of surplus and abundance. He would commend them for putting in their tithes and offerings, their fair share. But then he noticed a poor widow as she came and put in two copper coins, which had the purchasing power of approximately a penny. And he called his disciples and said, "Listen, you see all these people and what they are giving? This poor widow has put in more than all these who are contributing to the treasury."

This passage of scripture has invoked a great deal of discussion among church leaders because of mistaken interpretations. Some have wished that the text had been omitted from the scriptures, for it seems to proclaim the virtue of poverty. Others say the text implies that the church should be able to get along on the pennies, or on the nothings, that so many of us give. But none of this is the point which Jesus makes. The point Jesus makes is crystal clear. The amount we give is not important of itself. What is important is the amount we give in relation to what we have! The gift that counts is the gift that costs. Or conversely, the gift that costs is the gift that counts. When Jesus calls attention to the poor widow who has put in everything she had, he is calling his disciples and all who would follow him to costly giving.

How do we express our loyalty to God and to the church? How do we make up our personal and family budgets? Where on the list of expenditures do we have the church and Christian giving? Is it a top priority? Or is it something we consider only after our needs and desires are met. The creditors are usually first to be paid and the church last, because God does not press us as our creditors do. Needs must be met! But how shall we express our loyalty to God and to the church? The gift that counts is the gift that costs; and the gift that costs is the gift that counts.

Costly giving is the proper response to God's gift to us. In Paul's sermon at Areopagas, or Mars Hill (Acts 17:24-25), he said, "The God who made the world and everything in it, being Lord of heaven and earth, does not live in shrines made by man, nor is he served by human hands, as though he needed anything, since he himself gives to all men life and breath and everything." Life and breath, everything we are and have, these are gifts of God to us. It's costly! But the supreme example of God's costly giving is the gift of the Son, Jesus Christ, to save us from sin and death. Romans 5:6 says, "While we were still weak, at the right time Christ died for the ungodly." This is God's costly gift to us. Christ died and dies to save us and to give us hope. Costly giving is the way God chose to save the world. Costly giving is our proper response to God's love. When Jesus commended the poor widow, he was saying that a *fair share* is not enough; the tithe commanded by Moses is not enough. She gave all she had, everything. Costly giving which goes beyond duty and legalistic formulas is the proper response to God's love.

Costly giving is a pathway to liberation. The history of ethnic minority persons and communities in America is the story of struggle for freedom. Our churches have been at the vanguard, the forefront of that struggle. The church is the one institution in which we have experienced a measure of freedom. It has often been a weak institution, but it has led us in difficult times and brought us safe thus far. The church has proclaimed God's costly gift to us and God's will that all humankind, white and black and red and yellow and brown, male and female, shall be free. Ethnic minority local churches must be developed and strengthened for their continuing task. The 1980-1984 Missional Priority of The United Methodist Church was a relevant and valid response to this need. The danger we must guard against is developing a welfare mentality that could leave churches in a dependency relationship for the future. If that occurs, minorities will never be free. Costly giving, which will enable our churches to fulfill their ministry to themselves and their commitments to the world, is the only way to avoid the dependency relationship; it is a pathway to liberation.

One of the most inspiring experiences of my life has been my relationship with a minister—now retired—who preceded me in an earlier appointment. He was not considered a gifted preacher; he was never a district superintendent or pastor of what was thought to be a major church. He could not sing like an angel; he could not preach like Paul. Yet, he remained in that appointment for eight years and led three congregations in building completely new church buildings and a parsonage. As I have observed him over the years and have tried to discover his secret, I've concluded that, while he did not have a wealth of talent to give, he gave everything he had to the service of the Lord and to the work of the church. What we do in and through the church, and what we give to the church must always be prompted, not by some Mosaic or Levitical formula, but by a love and a loyalty to God which is based on God's love and loyalty to us. The poor widow gave all she had out of her love and loyalty to the religion of her forebears. If we follow her example, it will be costly. But it pays,. "a hundredfold now in this time . . . and in the age to come eternal life" (Mark 10:30). Costly giving is the proper response of the Christian to God's love; it is a pathway to liberation in this world; it is assurance of a home in glory. Amen.

THE STEWARDSHIP OF MONEY

David Adair
Oklahoma City, Oklahoma

Text: Wesleyan Sermon on "The Use of Money."

Biographical Sketch

David Adair is an American Indian born in Oklahoma in 1933. He served in the U.S. Army in Korea and was decorated with six Bronze Battle Stars. Following a career in advertising with his father, a business which they founded together, he entered the ministry. Rev. Adair has served for over eighteen years in Kansas and Oklahoma.

Presently Rev. Adair is the treasurer and secretary of the Oklahoma Indian Missionary Conference. He is an elder in full connection and a person who has been very active in stewardship in local churches and the conference program.

Rev. Adair lives in Oklahoma City with his family.

I purposely entitled this sermon "The Stewardship of Money," because I used to be a layman, and I can recall how it is to go into church and hear a sermon on money. It got right to me. The ones who were giving up to the suggested standard would seem comfortable, and could smile, and the others would have the look of puppies being scolded for a transgression. Stewardship sermons are most usually aimed toward a response of giving. This one is not.

Our Indian Missionary Conference requires over six hundred thousand dollars to be received from outside the conference each year. As conference treasurer, I am constantly trying to remind the conference that the stewardship of the conference will be its future—to become better stewards of the money God has given unto us.

What I really wish to talk about is the original Wesleyan concept of stewardship. You see, the Methodist movement was never intended to become a denomination; it was a kind of, well, method. Today, we might be called programmers. Stewardship was very much a part of the early discussions—but not in order to get more money for the Methodist movement, for its members were members of churches. The final assessment of stewardship, according to John Wesley, was, "Get all you can, save all you can, and give all you can."

Many think of stewardship as a matter of setting a biblical standard and then motivating persons to meet it as God instructs. This includes being involved in the mission of the church as Christ instructed. No church deserves more than it actually needs; and if a church does not spend its money reasonably for mission concerns, people should not feel obligated to give to it, just because it is a church.

Perhaps a look at Wesley's views at this point will help us to focus more clearly on what I wish to share.

1. Let's look at the first principle, "Earn all you can." Somehow this just doesn't sound like a central Christian principle. It seems to promote mammon. But wait a moment. You are a Christian. You have dedicated all of your life to God. But, in order to earn a living, you have to go out into the marketplace, and sell a portion of what you have already dedicated. You have to sell some of your life to educate your children, and feed them, and provide what it takes to live. Good stewardship demands that you get the most out of those portions of the life God has given you that you must sell. We must be good stewards of that which we sell. Some giving programs build on this very concept. I believe they are called "faith giving." People pledge to become better stewards of what they receive, and they pledge to increase toward a certain goal.

This whole concept of stewardship is based on the belief that God shares with us all resources that we have. Everyone. Every. It's not a portion of your life that belongs to God, not a *portion* of your goods, but *all*. If you were to give half of all that you have to the kingdom, and spend the rest foolishly, then you would be a foolish steward. A good Christian steward is one who knows what he or she has, how it was received, and plans to use it wisely for God's purpose.

Few people know what percent they will spend for food, or what the total cost of owning a car is. Good stewardship is developing a budget and sound system of managing the budget.

The very beginning of stewardship is to understand what money is, and how it is used, and how best to use it. Too often we sit down to work out our income tax, and see our total income, and ask where in the world did all that money go? What happened to it all?

We need to be very diligent, and never lose control of the resources that we have worked so hard to earn. We need to look at our society and see how it bleeds us. For example, all of us know that there is no cure for the common cold. But every drugstore has a section set aside for cold remedies, and we spend millions on them.

We waste millions in the improper use of the resources God has given.

We spend more to grow grass than food. We have so few years, and they are without price, but we spend them staring at the TV . . . time wasted that could have been spent in building love and understanding and reconciliation and peace. The beginning of Christian stewardship is to see all of life as a trust, and to get the very most from all of it. Earn all you can indeed! Use time to create. Hours that are not needed in earning money may be used to earn love and respect, and in learning the skills needed in Christian life. Make every moment count . . . and count every moment.

2. The concept of "saving all you can," to me, is a tremendous breakthrough in stewardship. Every payday, you know the things that you must do. You have to pay the loan company, so they can pay their salaries and stockholders. Pay the house rent, and utilities. Think of the thousands of people whose lives depend on your purchase of a car. The grocer needs your business, the children need their allowance. The insurance is due, and the paperboy must be paid. Buy gifts . . . put gas in the car . . . pay utilities! But how many of us ever pay ourselves?

In Wesley's day, there was no social security, and a person had to save for old age. I think this concept is even more appropriate today. Pay yourself. It's your life you are selling, your energy. Set aside an amount each payday, and say, this is mine . . . I earned it. For example, in business, you must invest in it in order to prosper. Your life is probably the greatest business you have. Invest in it. It's not selfish, you earned it. This goes for all things. Many people are caught up and spend their entire lives working for others, having no control over their own lives, no time for themselves. You can't dedicate your life to God if you have to spend most of it doing the bidding of others. Earn all you can, and control it. *You* control it! God will help you, if you trust and have the faith.

3. Wesley's third admonition is to "give all you can." This is very interesting to me. Though some would make giving a pharisaic tax, this has never been true. Since the very beginning, the work of the church or the tabernacle or temple has depended on giving. We are taxed to build a nation, or a highway. We are taxed to keep the railroads and the small farmer in business. A few years ago, we were surtaxed to pay for the war in Vietnam. But the church depends on your free gifts.

When we build the kingdom of God, we depend only on giving. The United Methodist Church raises hundreds of millions of dollars, all through giving. Missions all over the world are being funded because people give not only what was required, but much more. A church is assessed. A pastor may be told what to do or where he or she may live and serve, but givers come to church because they want to, and they give the amount they wish. A government may raise the tax, a retailer may raise the price, but the church still depends on the giver to give freely in love. To tell a church how much it should give is actually a waste of time. The amount of money given by a church depends on what is going on in terms of mission and outreach. It will depend on the extent to which its people are committed to Christ. No church is ever short on funds, only on commitment.

How is a church to survive, then, if its people never give? How long can it last? We are all aware of the problems of stewardship within the environment. We have lost the battle. Recently, I was near Lake Erie—one of several lakes that, two hundred years ago, were the biggest mass of pure, fresh water on the earth. Several years ago, industrial pollution had become so bad that no creature lived in these waters. Now, what about our stewardship of the environment of the kingdom? In Ireland, one Christian group kills another Christian group, and each does so in the name of Christ. A similar thing happens in the Middle East. Today, each of us will probably eat three meals. Some are too fat already. I really don't think any one of us will go hungry. Today, in Africa, however, children will die from starvation. Even within our own state, indeed our own city, there are children who will be hungry.

In a land of freedom, many of our people are in bondage to the bottle or drugs, or various other chains. What are we going to do about it? We must give. We must give of ourselves and our resources, and pledge that we are going to change things. For as we give money to the church, God is able to bless what we give, and it is increased a hundredfold.

Now is the day! Take stock of yourself. Who you are? What are you? What do you have? Dedicate it all to God and the kingdom, for stewardship is all of life. Christian stewardship is how you place a value on yourself and the work of God's kingdom. Amen.

GIVING AS SACRIFICIAL SHARING

Norval I. Brown
Maywood, Illinois

Text: 1 Kings 17:8-16—Elijah Raises the Widow's Son.

Biographical Sketch

Norval Ignatius Brown is a native of Brandywine, Maryland, a rural farming community, where he received his early education in the public schools. He continued his formal education at the University of Chicago, receiving the B.A. degree, and the Master of Divinity degree from Garrett-Evangelical Theological Seminary in 1979. He is pursuing the Doctor of Ministry degree at the University of Chicago.

He graduated valedictorian in his high school class, and received many outstanding awards and honors, such as Maroon Key honor in 1974 from the University of Chicago, the Sydney M. Katz scholarship award, and the Kyle Anderson baseball award.

Rev. Brown pastored several churches in Chicago before he received his present appointment as pastor of the Neighborhood United Methodist Church of Maywood, Illinois. He is married to the Rev. Ellen Renée Dill, and they live in Maywood.

The story of the pig and chicken is widely known. You may know it also. As they walked down the road one day, they came upon a church. In front of the church was a large sign that read, "Church Bazaar—Ham and Eggs for Sale." The hen turned to the pig and said, "See, my friend, even you and I can help the church." The pig looked at the hen and said, "Yes, my friend, but for you it is only a contribution, while for me it is a sacrifice."

This story points up the dilemma in which many Christians find themselves today. In a world with spiraling inflation, rising prices, and high unemployment, we find ourselves having to decide whether to contribute out of our abundance, or to give sacrificially to the church. Particularly as Blacks become more able to realize the American Dream—with nicer homes, greater blessings, and higher paying jobs—we must decide whether to be true givers to God and the church or mere contributors.

We are now living the American Dream, a dream that our forebears only dreamed about. We are so caught in the American Dream that our total lifestyle has been affected. We've reordered our priorities, and suddenly we do not give to the church as we should. Our heritage speaks of our fathers and mothers scraping together money from their meager earnings to build churches, communities, and colleges—but, for the most part, their sense of giving has been lost by the present generation.

At a recent finance committee meeting, we talked about a member who had ceased to come. It seemed that she was considered to be a good giver, based on the amount she put in the plate each Sunday. I pointed out to the committee that the amount put in the plate is truly not the standard by which one is termed a good giver. We had no knowledge of how much she was capable of giving. We didn't know how much it cost her to give.

As an illustration of a good giver, let us turn to the Gospel of Luke. We see that one day Jesus is sitting in the temple—one of the few gospel stories in which Jesus is not the prime character. He's sitting back observing, watching. He sits and watches the people as they come in the door. Some come in wearing long flowing robes, making a show of the money they give.

You can imagine that the gold glints in the air and as it tinkles into the treasury, the people turn around to see who dropped the money in the plate. And the people stand and smile as they are adored by the people who sit and watch. They are pleased with their contribution—and even more pleased with the adoration placed upon them. And then a woman enters—poor, widowed, alone—perhaps not knowing where her next meal will come from, probably having no means of support. To her, to be rich is just a dream that will never come true. Yet she walks up to the treasury just as everyone else. She stops, reaches deep into her pocket, and from the old, worn robe pulls out all that she has and drops it in the plate. Her gift is no mere contribution—even though it is not a great sum. She gives a sacrifice, because she gives all she has.

No one turns to notice her, there is no time for her to bask in the adoration of all those who are sitting there. But as she walks away, surely God smiles on her. Perhaps as she gives she thinks, "God has taken care of me, and now this money will help someone else." Or, "Lord, this is all that I have. I give you not only my money, but into your very hands, your most powerful and omnipotent hands, I am laying my life. I'm trusting that you will see me through." She gives out a deep sense of faith and gratitude—a faith that calls her to give back to God regardless of circumstances; a faith that tells her God who created the heavens and the earth will look after her.

Perhaps she sings as our slave parents sang:

> I'm going to trust in the Lord,
> I'm going to trust in the Lord,
> I'm going to trust in the Lord till I die.

She gave in response to her faith. And Jesus' response to her faith was, "Yes, this woman has given more than anyone else. The others contributed out of their abundance, but she gave her whole living." The giving was good because it was costly to the one who gave it. And that is the final determination of who indeed is a good giver. It is not how much we give, but it is how much it costs for us to give!

To give one's whole life, to let one's entire welfare be dependent upon God, this is the ultimate sacrifice—and the ultimate act of faith. And when we live by faith, we give more than contributions. We give according to the way God has blessed us and according to the level of our personal faith. We give with the assurance that:

> We've come this far by faith
> Leaning on the Lord
> Trusting in his Holy Word
> He's never failed me yet.

And God most assuredly cares for those who give their whole lives as an act of stewardship.

Let us examine Elijah's encounter with the widow of Zarephath. Elijah comes to her and says, "Make me some bread." But the widow responds, "I only have enough for the day for my son and me." And Elijah says to her, "Make it anyway." And recognizing Elijah as a man of God, she gives him no back talk, no argument. The soothing voice of Elijah assures her—and she finds faith. She fixes the bread for the man of God. He eats, she eats, her son eats—not just one meal, but they eat for days and days and days! And the meal does not run out, nor does the cruse of oil become empty! God was able to make what should have run out yesterday last for a lifetime. God's blessings flowed because the woman allowed herself to put her entire life in God's hands! God rewards our faithfulness.

Both these women gave in response to the way God had blessed them. Giving everything—the two coins or the day's supply of meal—was not an act of despair, or of giving up. It was the supreme act of faith, of dependence, of acknowledging God as the source of all goodness. Both gave out of a deep sense of gratitude. They gave to God as a way of saying, "Thank you, God, for all that you have done!" They understood that all things belong to God. They were giving back to God that which God had given them. Their giving was their stewardship. They "gave till it hurt"—and they experienced the joy of giving. We all have a need to give; to do so is to experience the joy of giving.

God has given, even as these women have given. God's faithfulness to creation led to the gift above every gift, God's only begotten Son, Jesus Christ. God responds to us out of faithfulness, and we should respond in like manner to God.

Our history is full of stories of people giving their all for the work of the church—great people such as Richard Allen, Mary McCleod Bethune, Howard Thurman, and hundreds of others. All one need do is look at the Black colleges, for example, begun when Blacks couldn't go to the Anglo institutions. And most of these schools began not out of anyone's generosity, but out of the meager earnings of former slaves, giving out of faithfulness to God who had nurtured and sustained them.

All we need to do is look at the Black churches across the denomination—churches which were built and maintained, not by the abundant contributions of rich benefactors, but which came about because a place of worship was the central focus in the life of a people. These people gave out of their poverty. The stewardship of giving was their hallmark.

This example must not be lost in the present age. We live the American Dream. But in so doing we may become as the people who enter the Temple—richly dressed, impressive in the amounts of money we give—but our giving is not always a faithful response to God's gifts to us. We do not give of our abundance, but rather from our leftovers.

Let us pray that our eyes shall be opened and our memories stirred. Let us recapture the faith and gratitude of our forebears, and let us reclaim our stewardship. As we recapture and reclaim, let us respond, not with contributions from our abundance. Let us respond out of our abundance—or our poverty—giving our whole lives to God. Let us give in faithfulness with the assurance that our God will supply all of our needs—today, tomorrow, and forever. Amen and Amen.

IS GOD IN YOUR BUDGET?

J. LaVon Kincaid, Sr.
Nashville, Tennessee

Text: Will a man rob God? Yet ye have robbed me. But ye say, Wherein have we robbed thee? In tithes and offerings. . . . Bring ye all the tithes into the storehouse, that there may be meat in mine house, and prove me now herewith, saith the Lord of hosts, if I will not open you the windows of heaven, and pour you out a blessing, that there shall not be room enough to receive it (Malachi 3:8-10, KJV).

Biographical Sketch

J. LaVon Kincaid, Sr. is a native of Bristol, Tennessee where he entered the ministry at the age of sixteen. LaVon holds the A.A. degree from Morristown College, Morristown, TN; the B.A. degree from Clark College of Atlanta, GA; and the Master of Divinity degree from the Interdenominational Theological Center, and Gammon Seminary of Atlanta, GA. Currently he is pursuing the Doctor of Ministry degree from Candler School of Theology and I.T.C. of Atlanta, GA.

Before assuming his present position in 1978 as Director of Stewardship, Board of Discipleship, The United Methodist Church, Nashville, Tennessee, he served as pastor of churches in Tennessee, Georgia, and most recently Kansas City, Missouri.

The Reverend Kincaid is experienced as a pastor, teacher, lecturer, author, civil rights leader, social activist, and radio and T.V. personality.

Many awards and honors have been bestowed upon him during his career of twenty-four years as a minister. He has been elected as Jurisdictional Conference delegate for two terms, 1976 and 1984. He is a member of the Missouri West Annual Conference of The United Methodist Church, where he serves on the Board of Ordained Ministry and Board of Discipleship. He has traveled widely and is experienced in ethnic minority local church stewardship and stewardship in the small membership church.

Reverend Kincaid lives in Nashville, Tennessee with his wife, Bobi, and sons, LaMar and J. LaVon, Jr.

Our message is taken from an exciting and important text found in the Old Testament. It is a text that every Christian must grapple with at some point or another. The prophet Malachi raises a fundamental and important question of stewardship, "Will a man rob God?" This is a question not only of stewardship but also of money management, and discipleship.

Therefore, as a subject from which to preach, I have chosen, "Is God in your budget?" This is a personal question and one that all Christians must answer in the affirmative, if we are to be faithful stewards of God's grace.

A story is told of a man who went each day to his backyard and uncovered his money which was buried in the ground. He would then put it back in the ground and cover it up again. To his shock and disappointment, on a particular day, he dug up the ground only to discover that his money was gone! He began to cry out in dismay. His neighbor heard his cry and came to his aid right away. Upon discovering his plight, the neighbor dropped his head, walked away, and said, "What's all the fuss about, you were not using the money for any good anyway! Maybe whoever got it will use it for some good."

While this is only a story, it points up the fact that our money is a resource, a gift from God, which is intended to be used properly to help ourselves, the church, and others. This is the essence of Christian money management: having enough to care for our needs and sharing what is left with God through the church offering.

In the Old Testament the question is raised in Malachi 3:8-10, "Will a man [or woman] rob God?" The prophet answers his own question when he declares, "Yet you have robbed me in your tithes." My friends, God has blessed us beyond merit, and yet many of us withhold from God our gifts of time, abilities, and especially our tithes. God has, however, instructed us in clear language to "bring . . . all the tithes into the storehouse that there may be meat in mine house, and prove me now . . . if I will not open you the windows of heaven and pour out a blessing that there shall not be room enough to receive."

What a wonderful promise God makes to all who will, in faith, obey this command. For each of us God has blessings stored, that we may never receive unless we are open and willing to put God first in our lives and affairs. In so doing, God is pleased and will bless us with greater blessings. Blessings such as health, happiness, joy, and Christian love for our neighbors all come from God alone.

Many of us do enjoy giving our gifts of money to the church, while others have failed to include God in the family or personal budget. When we fail to give to God, it is a form of "divine robbery." That is to say, whenever we do not put God and the church in the budget, we have indeed robbed God!

The family budget is a plan whereby all financial obligations are systematically met. This includes fixed expenses such as shelter, food, auto payments, utilities, and insurance. Adjustable expenses are also cared for through the budget. Without a budget, it is very difficult to function as a responsible adult or family unit. A family budget is a tool which is used to keep financial matters straight. It is a useful tool for directing our lives in putting God first in financial matters and giving.

The spiritual question before us is, Have we included God in our budget? Have we learned to give off the top? Have we discovered the real joy of giving? What does it mean to be giving persons? God would have all of us experience what is meant in the passage as recorded in John 3:16, "God so loved the world that he gave. . . ."

The story of the widow's mite, as recorded in Luke 21:1-4, points out to us that God desires our best when it comes to the giving of our gifts of money to the church. In so doing we find pleasure in the sight of God. Some, however, approach the giving of money to the church like the man who said to his friend, "I just throw my money up in the air; I figure that God will keep what God wants."

To include God in our budgets is good Christian stewardship. It is a form of planned spending. It is a thanks-giving to God for all the blessings we have received. To include God in our budget is an excellent way to say thank you to God for all our wonderful blessings.

As we grow in our spiritual understanding, we grow in our stewardship. One sign of spiritual growth is seen in the tithes and offerings we give back to God. When we become tithers, we experience the reality that we can't out-give God, no matter how hard we may try.

In 2 Corinthians 9, Paul teaches us that "He [or she] which soweth sparingly shall reap also sparingly; and he [she] which soweth bountifully shall reap also bountifully" (v. 6, KJV).

Let us be reminded of the words of the song which say, "The failure is not in God but in me." Whenever we fall short, however, God is always there to help us, and to restore.

We never come up short by putting God first in our life or budget. Let history be our witness. For example, Hannah of old, gave her first son back to God, and God gave her the greatest blessing of all. The widow gave only a mite (two pennies), but in so doing she received the blessing of Jesus and the honor of God, for she gave all that she had to give. Jesus, God's only Son, our rock in a weary land or shelter in a storm, the Rose of Sharon, the bright and morning star, Jesus . . . Jesus . . . Jesus, the perfect lamb of God, gave all that he had so that you and I might have a right to the tree of life! Greater love hath no one than this, that a man lay down his life for his friends. He didn't have to do it, but he did. He decided to give his life, just to save you and me.

In closing, may I remind you that God has instructed us to bring our tithes and offerings to the church, and by so doing receive blessings from on high. We do this not in order to be blessed, but because God has already blessed us greatly.

If you have not included God in your budget this year, will you do so by starting today? The first step is generally the hardest. However, if you take that first step, God will take two. God will open up the windows of heaven and pour out on you blessings from on high—because God is a God of love and mercy!

Trust in God, and believe in God's everlasting words. God will save your soul and give to you many wonderful blessings from the storehouse above. May God be in your budget each and every day. May the love of God surround you in every way. God has shown divine love to you. What will you do to show your love in return? Will you put God in your budget today? By so doing, you will be offering your "Thanks*giving" to God for the blessings you have received. Amen.

**CHICAGO BLACK METHODISTS
FOR CHURCH RENEWAL**
212 EAST 95th ST.
CHICAGO, ILLINOIS 60619